Charles Franklyn

A Man of Strong Opinions

PRO REGE PATRIA ET FAMILIA

Nicholas Groves

2023

Published by the Burgon Society (registered charity number 1137522)
http://www.burgon.org.uk/

ISBN: 978-1-8380679-0-8 (paperback), 978-1-8380679-5-3 (ebook)

The title page shows Franklyn's coat-of-arms, reproduced from Plate III of
The Bearing of Coat-Armour by Ladies.

This is the only known photograph of Charles Franklyn from the front, and shows him wearing the MD robe of Lausanne.
(From a colour transparency, reproduced by permission of Prof Len Newton.)

καὶ τόδε Φωκυλίδεω· τι πλέον γένος εὐγενὲς εἶναι
οἷς οὐτ ἐν μύθοις ἔπεται χάρις οὔτ ἐνὶ βουλῇ;

Phokylides says this: what's the use of blue blood
In people whose talk and opinions lack all grace?

– Phokylides (mid-C6 BCE; tr Peter Jay)

'... he felt that the enormous apparatus rank required a gentleman to erect around himself was like the massive armour that
had been the death warrant of so many saurian species.'

– John Fowles, *The French Lieutenant's Woman* (Chapter 38)

Contents

Preface

Charles A H Franklyn, Esq[re], MA, MD,[1] is a well-known figure in academic dress studies. This book started life when I rashly offered to start writing up the disparate material on him. He is best known for his *magnum opus Academical Dress*,[2] and as the designer of the robes for the Universities of Southampton and of Hull, and for Chichester Theological College – all of which were, according to his own assessment (in a phrase which has become something of a by-word among aficionados of the topic) 'most beautiful and dignified'. A very great deal of further material has come to light, and the longer I have worked on him, the less I like him. What started out as just a rather quirky old buffer has turned out to be a deeply unpleasant person.

It is the task of a biographer to write 'without fear of favour'. Many biographies flout this rule so far that they become hagiographies, and we are not allowed to see the undesirable aspects of their subjects' characters and behaviour. In the case of Franklyn, to do this would make a very slim volume indeed. Possibly there was an agreeable side to him, but if so, it was well hidden. The more one discovers, the less one likes him. As I have said, he was a very unpleasant person: obsessive and controlling, lacking in humour and self-awareness, irascible, self-important, and difficult to deal with. Why this was the case is not clear. Was it the result of his upbringing, or was he over-compensating for a naturally retiring character? Is it possible that he was to some extent autistic? It has been difficult not to be judgmental, but a good deal of the time, even allowing for differing social norms over time, it has been impossible to be otherwise.

This is not a strict biography, however, as it seems better to arrange the material thematically. I start with chapters on his family and background, and an overview of his life, and one on his character. These are followed by a discussion of his academic awards, and his involvement with the University of London. The main chapter discusses his schemes of academic dress, including attributing some early schemes to him that have not previously been known about. This is followed by a short chapter on his heraldic work: I have looked only at such items as were accepted. In correspondence with

---

[1] His preferred form of address over Dr Charles Franklyn.
[2] His preferred version of the term, which he was not above correcting at every possible opportunity.

the various institutions with which he worked, he always says that the study of academic dress or of heraldry (whichever was in question) had been his life's work: clearly this meant more to him than his medical career. The book closes with a discussion of his Will and its stipulations.

It is fortunate that we have a good deal of correspondence both to and from Franklyn, as well as several personal accounts from those who met him, and I am grateful to those who have shared information with me. In particular, material is coming to light at some of the 1960s universities where he attempted to get appointed as the robe designer: I am sure there is more to come to the surface, but I am fairly certain it will replicate what we already have. The exception is the University of Essex, where he was gravely offended not to be considered, and that correspondence we do have. His letters are a challenge to read, as his handwriting was notoriously poor (one university took to having typed transcripts made), and I am grateful for my palæographic training, which has made the task somewhat easier! There are, nonetheless, passages which defeat decipherment.

I am conscious that I have not looked at most of his genealogical works. I can but plead lack of time, and the difficulty of finding copies to consult, owing to their very small print runs. But as they were, presumably, intended for use only within the relevant families, I think we have not missed much. The question remains of how he came by the commissions to compile them in the first place.

I am grateful to Dr Alex Kerr for the subtitle 'a man of strong opinions' – to which might well be added '... most of them wrong'.

NWG
Norwich, 25 August 2022 (Charles Franklyn's 126th birthday).

Acknowledgments

This work has been a good while in the making, and could not have reached this stage without assistance from a number of people, among whom the following have been instrumental:

Ms Penelope Baker (archivist of Exeter College, Oxford); Dr Richard Baker; John Balsdon; Sqn-Ldr Alan Birt; Arthur Casey; Prof Bruce Christianson; Dr Paul Coxon; the Revd Edmund Egglestone; the Revd Dr Peter Galloway; Prof William Gibson; the Revd Philip Goff; Dr John Horton; Prof William Hughes; Dr Nicholas Jackson; Dr Alex Kerr; Prof Len Newton; Dr Andrew North; Robin Richardson (J Wippell and Co); the late Dr George Shaw and the late Dr Mary Shaw.

I am particularly grateful to Prof Gibson and Dr Kerr for reading and commenting on the initial draft.

I am also grateful to a large number of friends and colleagues, both within and without the Burgon Society, who have been willing to listen to my thoughts, discuss them, and (not infrequently) express horror at this 'troublesome old gentleman'.

As is so often the case these days, my task has been made infinitely easier by Google Books, Ancestry.com, and the British Newspaper Archive. And I might note that the advent of Covid-19 provided a good deal of time during which I could concentrate on finally pulling all the information together.

Credits

The photographs of Dr Franklyn on pages iii and 60 were taken by Prof Len Newton, and are reproduced by kind permission.

The letter on page 23 is reproduced by kind permission of Arthur Casey.

The photographs of Franklyn's Lincoln-Jefferson MA hood on page 32 and his Malaya MA hood on page 61 are reproduced by kind permission of John Balsdon.

The photographs of the London laws and medicine gowns on page 38 are reproduced by kind permission of the Revd Philip Goff.

The London BMus robes on page 42, the [s2], [f3] and [f5] hoods on pages 46 and 46, the Chichester Theological College hood on page 59, and the Philosophical Society fellowship hood on page 81, belong to the Burgon Society's collection, and the photographs were kindly provided by the Archivist, Chris Williams.

The photographs of Dr Franklyn wearing Southampton and Hull hoods pages 63 and 65 are reproduced from the fifth edition of Haycraft's *Degrees and Hoods*.

The picture of Franklyn's arms on the title page and on page 97 are reproduced from *The Bearing of Coat-Armour by Ladies.*

The arms of St Peter's College, Oxford, on page 103, and those of Bridgnorth Borough Council, on page 106, are reproduced from Wikimedia Commons under a Creative Commons Attribution-ShareAlike 3.0 licence.

The British Transport Commission emblem on page 105 is reproduced by kind permission of David Slater.

The Author

Dr Nicholas Groves is a graduate of the Universities of Wales (Aberystwyth and Lampeter), London, East Anglia, and York, a Fellow of the Royal Historical Society, and a founding Fellow of the Burgon Society. He is the editor of *Shaw's Academical Dress.* He has taught in secondary schools and in Continuing Education, and is now a freelance lecturer and writer. His other works on academic dress include booklets on the robes of St David's College, Lampeter (UWL, 2000; second edition 2022) and the University of East Anglia (Burgon Society 2005), on the hoods of theological colleges (Burgon Society 2004), and music colleges (with John Kersey, Burgon Society 2002), as well as several articles in the Society's Transactions. His designs for revisions and additions to the robes of the University of Malta won an international competition, and he has designed robes for a number of other institutions. His other biographical work includes publications on Sarah Glover (London, 2006) and William Gilly (Norwich, 2014).

1 Family and Background

Charles Aubrey Hamilton Franklyn was born in Brentwood on 25 August 1896, the son of Captain (later Major) Aubrey Hamilton Franklin (1869–1921) and his wife Ethel Mary Franklin (née Gray; 1871–1937).[1] In the 1901 Census, they were living at Gleadowe Lodge, Queen's Road, Brentwood.[2] Both parents were Essex people: his father was born at Ingatestone (although, as we shall see, the origins of the family are less clear-cut), and his mother in Chelmsford.[3] There were two children recorded in this Census: Charles, and his sister, Irene Hamilton, who was three years younger. The family employed a nurse, a cook, and a house-parlourmaid. The area was well-to-do: occupations of neighbours were corn-factor, fishmonger, grocer, a retired architect, and a newspaper proprietor (John Collingridge). All had servants. In 1902, the family moved to Furze Hall, Horsell, in Surrey.[4] This is in fact a large farmhouse on the Wickham Road, 'Probably timber-framed originally, but now clad in brick'.[5] Between 1908 and 1918 they had moved to Liskeard Gardens in Blackheath: at present the exact date and reason is not known.

The change of spelling of the surname took place in 1932. This is recorded in an MS corrigendum slip stuck in to copy number fourteen of the Short Genealogical History, now in the possession of Arthur Casey. It reads:

> amended 24 Dec: 1936.
> The author, Dr Charles AH Franklyn, resumed the ancient and original and fundamentally correct form of patronymic FRANKLYN (in lieu of the debased form, 'Franklin') from 1 Jan: 1932. This was embodied in a Statutory Declaration to that effect in May 1934, duly lodged with The General Medical Council, and other Colleges and Universities, and at HM College of Arms.

---

[1] CAHF changed the spelling of his name to Franklyn in 1933, as a result of his research into his own family history, although it is also the year his marriage was annulled. To avoid confusion, I shall refer to him as 'Franklyn' throughout.

[2] This information from the 1901 Census.

[3] Franklyn was very proud of his Essex ancestry, giving it as one reason why he should have designed the robes for the University of Essex: 'an Essex-born man with an Essex descent of 300 years!' (Letter to Charles Leatherland, 13 December 1963.) See below, page 79.

[4] Charles A H Franklyn, *A Short Genealogical & Heraldic History of the Families of Frankelyn of Kent and Franklyn of Antigua & Jamaica, B.W.I.*, E O Beck (1930). Hereafter *SGH*.

[5] https://historicengland.org.uk/listing/the-list/list-entry/1233551 (accessed 31 August 2020).

Other members of the family, including his former wife, seem to have stuck with the former spelling. The fact that spelling conventions, particularly with the interchange of i and y, were relatively fluid until the eighteenth century seems to have escaped him. So far as 'fundamentally correct' goes, he might have adopted the form used invariably by Chaucer, 'Frankeleyn', or even ffranklyn, using the old convention of a double f for an upper-case F.[6]

The 1911 Census lists the family at 93, Carlisle Road, Hove, a ten-room residence, with a nurse and a 'servant'; possibly they were on holiday.

There was by this time also a third sibling, Harold Gordon, born in 1904 at Horsell, in Surrey. He became an engineer, and took the Aviator's Certificate of the Royal Aero Club in 1947, at which time he was working as an engineer at the Limmer and Trinidad Lake Asphalt Company, of Carnwath Road, Fulham. He died in Surrey in 1982, and was unmarried. Irene married Theobald Owens in 1931: at the time of Owens' death in 1984 they were living in Sussex.[7] They had a daughter, Margaret Ann.[8]

The family's origins are given in the *Short Genealogical & Heraldic History of the families of Frankelyn of Kent and Franklyn of Antigua & Jamaica, B.W.I.*[9] He traces the family back to a John Franklyn, resident in Antigua in 1678, and who possibly emigrated in 1654,[10] but cannot go any further back.[11] His reason for saying 1654 is given in note 2 on page 62: the name occurs in the pay roll of General Robert Venables as a 'chirugeon mate'. It would seem likely that he gained a grant of land, and became a planter.

Franklyn's great-grandfather, Henry (1840–99) was born in Kingston, Jamaica, and married (1834) and died (1857) there.[12] The couple had nine children, and his widow brought them to England in 1859. His grandfather Charles (1842–87) was therefore born in Kingston. He had two sons, Herbert Charles Temple Franklin, who became a clergyman, and Aubrey Hamilton Franklin, father of the subject of this work.[13]

Franklyn was, presumably, named after his paternal grandfather, Charles Franklin, who, in 1881, was living at The Lindens, Putney, and described himself as a 'general practitioner'. He was initially in practice in Brentwood, moving to Putney in 1876. He seems to have formed a role model, as he was also educated at Tonbridge School, and became a medical practitioner. He

---

[6] It is worth a note in passing that the name means 'a landowner of free but not noble birth', P H Reaney, *A Dictionary of British Surnames*, Routledge and Kegan Paul, London (1958), page 125 sv 'Franklin...'.

[7] Theobald David Cogswell Owens, 1899–1984. In 1924 he was a passenger on the Narkdua to India, described as Captain.

[8] She registered Franklyn's death. She must have been about fifty when she did so, and had Owens as her surname, so was unmarried.

[9] Hereafter *SGH*.

[10] Franklyn, *SGH*, page 61.

[11] Ibid., page 61.

[12] It is possible that he is the Henry Franklin who claimed compensation for slaves in 1836: http://wwwdepts-live.ucl.ac.uk/lbs/person/view/42923 (accessed 31st August 2020).

[13] For further discussion of the family's origins, see Chapter 7.

died at the age of forty-five, from heart-failure while recuperating at Brighton, and was buried at Putney Cemetery: Franklyn chose to be buried in his grave. There is a memorial window in All Saints' Church.

His grandfather's brother, Herbert Charles Temple Franklin, incurred Franklyn's displeasure. His entry in the *Short Genealogical & Heraldic History* tells us that he was ordained, and was in due course appointed Rector of Swainswick near Bath, a living in the gift of his old College, Oriel.

> He was a great friend of Julia Charlotte, Dowager Countess of Shannon, to who he left in his will which was proved in the PPR 1916, he left the great bulk of his property, amounting to over £10 000, thus alienating from the family his father's and his mother's money, in direct contravention of the wishes of the original devisors.[14]

His maternal grandfather, Walter Gray, of Phoenix House, New London Road, Chelmsford, was a brewer and maltster, employing, in 1881, twenty-six men.[15] So Franklyn's background hovered in that very grey area between the 'professional' (the medical grandfather) and the 'merchant trade' (the brewer grandfather).

His father clearly wished to be a 'gentleman', but seems not quite to have succeeded. He listed himself in the 1901 Census as 'member of the Stock Exchange' and 'Army Officer: Captain in the First V[olunteer] B[attalion], the Essex Regiment'. He was educated at King's College School in London.[16] Intended for service in the Navy, he was prevented from doing so by an attack of typhoid fever. He joined the Stock Exchange when his father died in 1887. He became a Member in 1890, and from 1902–1920 he was a partner in the firm Gunn & Franklin.[17] His naval aspirations were carried out as a member of the RNVR, until it was disbanded 'in the 'nineties',[18] when he joined the Essex Regiment (Volunteers), becoming a Captain. He was recommissioned as a Captain in the Royal West Kent Territorial Force in 1913, and served in the 1914–19 War, rising to Major. Owing to regulations to do with his being over forty, he was unable to be promoted as Lt-Colonel, nor go to France with his battalion. He was, however, posted there in 1917 as a Camp Commandant, being invalided home in January 1918 as a result of gas, which impaired his health. He was granted the rank of Major in 1918.

In 1891 his occupation was listed simply as 'Stock Exchange' – with 'broker' crossed through by the enumerator and 'agent' substituted, and in 1911 as

---

[14] Franklyn, *SGH*, page 78. The National Probate Calendar reveals that he left £10 211 16s 10d, with the dowager countess being granted probate. This is about £697 400 in 2020.

[15] 1881 Census. On the Grays, see further Chapter 7.

[16] Franklyn, *SGH*, page 78.

[17] Ibid., page 78.

[18] It is hard to see what he means by this. The Royal Naval Reserve (RNR) was created in 1859, but the Royal Naval Volunteer Reserve (RNVR) not until 1903. Neither was disbanded as such, but they were merged in 1958.

'Stockjobber'.[19] It would seem that his father needed (for whatever reason) a military title in order to fix his social status. However, this use was inappropriate. Debrett states on its page about the use of titles by retired and former officers:

> Field marshals whether promoted while serving or in retirement continue to use this rank. Other regular officers who attained the substantive rank of captain and above may use, and be addressed by, their rank on retirement from the Army. It is not accepted practice for retired officers of the Reserve to use or be addressed by, their rank on retirement unless employed in a civilian capacity in a Ministry of Defence establishment.[20]

The use of the rank by territorial officers outside military situations, even when in employment, is also not regarded as correct.

Aubrey Franklin died in 1921, aged fifty-two, and was buried at Charlton Cemetery, near Blackheath. Doubtless his wartime injuries led to his early death.

Ethel Franklin died in difficult circumstances in 1937. She had been unwell for some time, and had been in St Thomas' Hospital for 'a serious operation', and had been depressed as she had lost her sight. She died after falling from a window of the house in Blackheath, and a verdict of 'suicide while of unsound mind' was recorded.[21]

Certainly Franklyn himself was very touchy about his status: he rigorously maintained that there were but two 'professions' – medicine and the law – and that everything else (such as school-mastering, dentistry, etc) was an 'occupation' or 'trade'.[22] But his medical grandfather was not fully 'professional', as, although he had studied at Guy's Hospital, he held no degree: he was, according to *SGH*, a Licentiate of the Society of Apothecaries (LSA)[23] and a Member of the Royal College of Surgeons (MRCS), and as such not even strictly entitled to the courtesy title of 'Doctor' accorded to (or, more accurately, assumed by) Members and Fellows of the Royal College of Physicians.[24] A letter from

---

[19] On his marriage certificate (see below) Franklyn described his father as 'Major (TF) and Member of the Stock Exchange'.

[20] http://www.debretts.com/forms-address/professions/armed-forces/army/retired-and-former-officers#sthash.BCNFGaVo.dpuf (accessed 13 June 2015).

[21] *The Essex Chronicle*, 15 January 1937, page 7.

[22] Arthur B Casey, 'Academic Dress: Personal Reminiscences', *Transactions of the Burgon Society* 8 (2008) 151–156, page 153.

[23] Franklyn, *SGH*, page 77. In one of his Census returns he lists himself as LAH. This was a qualifying medical diploma awarded externally by the Apothcaries' Hall, which was in Dublin, until recognition was lost in 1971. However, this may be an error for LSA as the Apothecaries in London also have a Hall. It would be interesting to know why (if he did) he chose an Irish qualification. LAH replaced the term 'Master Apothecary' in 1826. Under the Medical Act of 1858 the Apothecaries' Hall was recognised as one of the official awarding bodies of medical qualifications, and the LAH was one of the recognised qualifications for a medical practitioners in the British Isles. Licentiateships awarded after 1971 were honorary awards.

[24] This seems to have come about as all FRCPs originally had to be MDs of Oxford or Cambridge.

Franklyn, on lined file-paper, to the first Vice-Chancellor of the University of Warwick has, scrawled across the top: 'Please address letters as printed hereon', with a printed letter-heading stuck on with Sellotape, which reads 'Charles AH Franklyn, Esq, MA, MD, FLS', (and not, therefore, to 'Dr Charles Franklyn', which presumably they had previously used), again revealing his insecurity about his social standing:[25]

'Esquire' was, of course, a rank within the gentry, but who exactly was an esquire was to great extent a matter of opinion. Charles Boutell stated in 1899:

> *Esquire* – A rank next below that of Knight. Besides those Esquires who are personal attendants of Knights of Orders of Knighthood, this title is held by all attendants on the person of the Sovereign, and all persons holding the Sovereign's commission being of military rank not below Captain; also, by general concession, by Barristers at Law, Masters of Arts and Bachelors of Law and Physic.[26]

His own view on the status is given on page 19 of *A Short Genealogical and Heraldic History*:

> Note: the description 'Esqre.' is used throughout this book in its ancient and strictly legal and correct interpretation, namely, a person entitled to bear Arms, viz., Armiger, Scutifer, Esquire. The courtesy title is also accorded to the sons of Peers, of Baronets, and of Knights, and their eldest sons in perpetuity, Companions of Orders of Knighthood, Commissioned Officers of H.M. Services, J.P's of Counties whilst in commission, and so on, unless previously qualified by bearing Arms. The use of the description 'gentleman', as advocated by Fox-Davies, as a title, by those who bear Arms is incorrect, as gentleman is synonymous with Nobleman or untitled 'Noblesse' alike: all are members of the same class differenced only by degrees of rank.

As will become apparent later,[27] Franklyn's view of who was a 'gentleman' was totally wound up with the right to bear arms, to the point of obsession – and as so often, may well be his own opinion being paraded as fact. His own arms were held by right of a retrospective and confirmatory grant to his great-grandfather, and he was extremely irritated that no-one in his mother's family had seen the need to get a retrospective grant. There is a section of the

---

Thus it was assumed that all Fellows were necessarily Doctors; from there, the use of the courtesy title of 'doctor' for all medical practitioners (except surgeons) spread, rather as the use of 'vicar' for any member of the clergy has.

[25] Letter, Franklyn to J Butterworth, 22 September 1964; reproduced in: Nicholas Jackson, 'The Development of Academic Dress in the University of Warwick', *Transactions of the Burgon Society* 8 (2008) 10–59, page 14.

[26] Charles Boutell, *English Heraldry*, Gibbings and Co., London (1899), page 120.

[27] See further Chapter 7.

codicil to his will dealing with the heraldic bearings of his grand-niece, and also with causing her future husband to acquire a grant if he did not already have arms.[28]

So, according to Boutell, Franklyn was entitled to be addressed as 'Esq' by virtue of his MB (and possibly his honorary MA), whereas he was claiming it by his right to bear arms – a right which, as we shall see, he acquired for himself and his ancestors in the 1930s.[29] But he was kicking against the pricks: 'Esquire' had become universal in the United Kingdom by the mid-twentieth century, with no distinction in status being perceived between 'Mister' (the historic form of address for Gentlemen, the rank next below) and 'Esquire'. 'Esquire' had come to be used generally as the default title for all men who did not have a grander title when addressing correspondence – thus one imagines that 'Doctor' would outrank 'Esquire'. In the 1970s, the use of the post-nominal Esq started to decline, and by the end of the twentieth century most people had stopped using it and used Mr instead. He was also insistent that he be referred to as a 'physician', and not as a 'medical practitioner'.[30] Again, this harks back to long-vanished distinctions, where a physician was specifically one who held a bachelor's or doctor's degree in Physick (Medicine), whereas a medical practitioner did not necessarily do so – and in many cases, might even be utterly unqualified.[31]

Tonbridge School

Franklyn attended Edinburgh House preparatory school, in Lee-on-the-Solent, from 1906 to 1910.[32] Founded as The Royal Naval School in 1895, when the Navy set up its own school in 1905, they asked the Headmaster to rename it. Being a Scotsman, he chose the name Edinburgh House, so it had just been renamed when Franklyn was sent there. After various moves and amalgamations with other schools, it is now at New Milton, Hants, called the Ballard School, and takes pupils up to the age of sixteen.

In September 1910, at the age of fourteen, he was sent to Tonbridge School. One particular tradition of the school is that of the 'House Square': a piece of silk awarded by the House to a boy, which may be turned into a House waistcoat, etc, each house having its own colours. Franklyn's House was Ferox Hall, the colours of which are orange and yellow.[33] It is not known if Franklyn was ever awarded one, and thus sported such a garment, but

---

[28] See further Chapter 8.

[29] See pages 95–100.

[30] Personal communication, Sqn-Ldr Alan Birt.

[31] Whether deliberately or otherwise, his niece recorded him as a 'medical practitioner' when she registered his death.

[32] Franklyn, *SGH*, page 80.

[33] *Tonbridge School Register, 1910*. The Hall, which is a Tudor house, already bore the name when the School acquired it. It is the Latin word for 'ferocious' – possibly quite apt when considering some of CAHF's pronouncements!

he frequently said that his interest in academic dress started at school – as indeed it has for many others.

His medical grandfather, Charles Franklin, had attended the school, though his father did not do so: it is not known why this was.

Military Service

On leaving school in 1914, Franklyn proceeded to St Thomas' Hospital, where he matriculated in January 1915, to read medicine.[34] This was interrupted by war service: called up in 1915, he served from 25 November 1915 to 9 February 1919[35] in France as a Lieutenant in the Royal Garrison Artillery (Special Reserve of Officers, Supplementary).[36] His service record is set out in *SGH*, page 80 as follows:

> 24 November 1915: 2nd lieutenant RGA (SR);
> 1 July 1917: lieutenant RA;
> 6 June 1916 to 6 February 1919: in France:
>> June 1916–May 1917: anti-aircraft service, RA, on the Somme;
>> May 1917–February 1919: 2nd army, northern front;
>> 1918: commanded 15th AA section, Great Advance.

The Corps was disbanded on 1 April 1920, and he was 'granted the rank of lieutenant.'[37] Is this another cause of his prickliness: that he had had a relatively easy war, while his father was invalided out, and with a higher rank?

It is perhaps strange that, as a medical student, he did not volunteer to join a medical unit.[38] But he doubtless saw it incumbent upon him, as a gentleman, to take a commission, which possibly he could not have done in a medical unit, as he was not yet qualified.

During the Great War officers could be commissioned into numerous different forces, and for an officer in the RGA it was possible in the following ways:

1. as a 2nd Lieutenant in the regular RGA
2. as a Temporary 2nd Lieutenant in the regular RGA
3. as a 2nd Lieutenant in the RGA, Territorial Force
4. as a 2nd Lieutenant in the Special Reserve of Officers

---

[34] His grandfather had trained at Guy's.

[35] Dates from his Will. *SGH* gives 24 November 1915.

[36] He was awarded the Victory and British Medals (Medal card, National Archives, WO 372/7/146900).

[37] Franklyn, *SGH*, page 80.

[38] This was the choice of some objectors, such as the composer Ralph Vaughan Williams, who became a stretcher-bearer. Many of them put their lives in as much danger as if they had been combatants.

5. as a 2nd Lieutenant in the Special Reserve of Officers – Supplementary to Regular Units or Corps.
6. as a 2nd Lieutenant in the Reserve of Officers
7. as a 2nd Lieutenant in the Militia.[39]

The Royal Garrison Artillery (RGA) was an arm of the Royal Artillery that was originally tasked with manning the guns of the British Empire's forts and fortresses, including coastal artillery batteries, the heavy gun batteries attached to each infantry division, and the guns of the siege artillery. From 1914, when the army possessed very little heavy artillery, the RGA grew into a very large component of the British forces on the battlefield, being armed with heavy, large-calibre guns and howitzers that were positioned some way behind the front line and had immense destructive power. The corps name was discontinued in 1924, when the RGA was re-amalgamated into the Royal Artillery.[40]

'A Physician, not a medical practitioner'

He returned to St Thomas' in February 1919, and was admitted MRCS and LRCP (the 'Conjoint Diplomas') in January 1923, and was registered as a medical practitioner on 26 January 1923.[41] He graduated MB,BS(Lond), with distinction in physiology, the following year, and he was 'created' MD at the University of Lausanne on 12 March 1925.[42]

After qualifying, he followed a somewhat peripatetic existence. In 1927 he was still living at his mother's house in Blackheath;[43] in 1929 in the Precincts of the Savoy;[44] in 1931 in Folkestone;[45] in 1935 in Lincoln,[46] where he served also as the prison doctor. According to *SGH*, he had posts as follows:

> 1923–25: several locums.
> 1925–30: partner with Cecil Ernest Millington Lewis, and Philip Rutherford Boswell, at Bickley in Kent. (Bickley is near Bromley, so an easy journey from Blackheath.)
> January 1931–'late 1932': assisted Dr JGP Murray at Folkestone.

---

[39] http://1914-1918.invisionzone.com/forums/index.php?showtopic=21510
[40] Note that CAHF says 1920.
[41] *The Medical Register* for 1927. Until 1937, the majority (85%) of London medical students obtained registration on the basis of the 'Conjoint', and not the MB,BS, though about half went on to obtain the degrees. Registration on the basis of the MB,BS for the majority did not happen until the revised regulations of 1973. (L P LeQuesne, *Medicine*, in: *The University of London and the World of Learning, 1836–1986*, ed. by F M L Thompson, Hambledon (1990), page 135, note 31.)
[42] Thus *SGH*, page 80. See further, Chapter 3.
[43] 23, Liskeard Gardens; *The Medical Register* for 1927. His father had died in 1921.
[44] Marriage certificate.
[45] 154, Sandgate Road; *The Medical Register* for 1931, and also the annulment papers, in which the house is called 'Greenbank'.
[46] 34, Queensway, off the Wragby Road; *The Medical Register* for 1935. This is 'The Corner House' of his bookplate.

> most of 1933: temporary MO on the P&O line (see below,
> page 10)
> Dec 1933: partner with Douglas Edward Darbyshire, at Lin-
> coln, and MO to Lincoln Prison from July 1934. This must
> have ended in 1940, when he went up to Oxford.

His medical speciality was blood pressure, for which he had a single prescription: a low salt diet.[47] He was on a low-sodium diet, and apparently kept his cats on one also.[48] He had an underlying problem with high blood pressure himself, and it was a contributory factor to his death.

Do you take this woman ...?

Franklyn married, on 16 July 1929, Erica Milly Bolton, at the Savoy Chapel: he was resident within the Precinct of the Savoy at the time, though exactly where is unclear. The ceremony was conducted by Henry Albert Wilson, the Bishop of Chelmsford.[49] The chapel, which belongs to the Sovereign as Duke of Lancaster, and is extra-diocesan, was noted in the eighteenth century as a place where marriages might occur 'outside of the usual parameters of ecclesiastical law' at that time – i.e., without banns or licence – and was referred to in Evelyn Waugh's *Brideshead Revisited* as 'the place where divorced couples got married in those days – a poky little place'. However, as we might expect, Franklyn was regularly married, after banns. But we may wonder how he came to be married there in the first place, and this is not known. The Precinct of the Savoy was a civil parish between 1866 and 1922, when it was abolished: the marriage took place seven years later. He was also still employed in medical practice at Bickley.

Erica Bolton was the daughter of Felix Dickeson Bolton of Bromley, a wholesale provision merchant.[50] She was born in 1906, and was thus ten years younger than Franklyn, and was twenty-three at the time of the marriage. As we have seen, Franklyn was in practice at Bickley, near Bromley, from 1925 to 1930, and doubtless they met there.

The marriage was annulled in 1933, Mrs Franklin's incapacity to consummate the marriage being cited as the grounds for annulment: she was twenty-

---

[47] Personal communication, the late Dr George Shaw.
[48] Casey, 'Academic Dress: Personal Reminiscences', page 152.
[49] Copy of marriage certificate among the annulment papers (see below). Wilson (1876–1961) was ordained in 1899; curate of Christ Church, Hampstead, 1899–1904; Vicar of Norbiton 1904–15; Rector of Cheltenham 1915–28; Bishop of Chelmsford 1929–50. He was consecrated bishop in January 1929, so had been a bishop for but a few months when he officiated at Franklyn's wedding. The reason for his doing so remains unknown; he was certainly not the Chaplain of the Savoy Chapel. Ironically, a proposal in 1944 to expedite divorce by allowing the cases to be heard in magistrates' courts, rather than higher ones, prompted his strenuous objection: 'the landslide in sexual morals' meant that Christianity was 'hanging by a thread in this country today'. ('Religion: Pretty Pass', *Time Magazine*, 31 June 1944.) Franklyn's parents were married in what was to become, in 1914, Chelmsford Cathedral (*SGH*, page 79).
[50] Census, 1911.

seven.[51] The petition is quite explicit, and alleges that 'at the time of the said marriage [she] was and ever since has been and still is incapable of permitting the Petitioner to consummate the said marriage by reason of her incapacity frigidity and defective parts of generation', and both were required to undergo a physical examination to prove the fact. She appears not to have contested the case, even though she continued to call herself Mrs Franklin (with the original spelling).[52] She died in 1984.

It is, perhaps, typical of Franklyn that he went for a full annulment, and not a simple divorce, although grounds for divorce in the 1930s were far more difficult to obtain than they are now, and non-consummation does mean that the marriage was not completed. One can hardly imagine him compromising his dignity by going through the then-standard farce of being 'accidentally' caught in flagrante with a co-operative chambermaid in a Brighton hotel!

Franklyn's own opinion on the marriage is in a letter of 22 December 1936 to a Mr Carr.[53] The relevant section reads:

> If publication had been delayed a few months, I should have expunged from the work a certain event which I was about to have 'washed out'. I endured 3 years of it & really couldn't go on any longer, participating in a fraud. She was abnormal & [?]evil could be ..., so I broke up the home, let the house (hers) for £170 p.a., sold my partnership, went home, & at once filed my petition. It was granted, & the whole thing annulled, in March 1933: undefended. I had a trip round the world shortly afterwards, & then came home Dec '33, & joined an old St Thomas' man, DE Darbyshire.[54]

Quite what the 'fraud' was is unclear: possibly her inability to consummate the marriage, which she had not disclosed beforehand.[55] The 'trip round the world' was of course his temporary appointment as an MO. He summarizes the itinerary in *SGH*: he 'visited Gibraltar, Tangier, Port Said, went through the Canal to Aden, and visited Bombay, Ceylon, and all round Australia from Perth to Brisbane and back.' So, not quite round the world, then, nor, arguably, 'a trip', as that implies pleasure, and he was working.

Despite this, he decided after ten years, to marry again, this time to Elisabeth Mary Ramsden, daughter of George Taylor Ramsden, of Boston Spa, Yorks. The marriage, which was to 'take place very quietly, by licence', was

---

[51]National Archives, Kew: Divorce Court File: 4553. Appellant: Charles Aubrey Hamilton Franklin. Respondent: Erica Milly Franklin otherwise Erica Milly Bolton. Type: Husband's petition for/of nullity.

[52]I am grateful to Dr Nicholas Jackson for this information.

[53]I am grateful to Arthur Casey for a copy of this letter, which is in his possession. 'The publication' is *SGH*; I can find no reference to the marriage in it.

[54]Letter, Franklyn to Carr, 22 December 1936; in possession of Arthur Casey. The ellipsis marks an illegible passage, something all too common with CAHF's writing. Other correspondents were known to have made typed transcripts! 'Home' here means Blackheath.

[55]One dearly wishes to hear the story from her side.

announced in the Yorkshire Post late in 1946.[56] However, it came to nothing, and in February the following year it was announced that it was not to happen.[57] One wonders what had happened: had Miss Ramsden or her mother perhaps been talking to the first Mrs Franklin? GT Ramsden was a Captain in the Territorial Army, had been Unionist MP for Elland 1918–22, and had died in 1936. The initial announcement, which appeared in the 'Court and Personal' column, is worth quoting in full, as one can see Franklyn in his full pomp:

> A marriage has been arranged, which will take place very quietly by licence early in the New Year, between Charles Aubrey Hamilton Franklyn, MD, FLS, of Hassocks, Sussex, elder son of the late Aubrey Hamilton Franklyn, esq, Major, TF Res, late of Furze Hall, Horsell, Surrey, and Elizabeth Mary (Betty), eldest daughter of the late George Taylor Ramsden, esq, MA(Cantab), JP, Captain, TF Res, of Bramham House, Boston Spa, Yorks, and Mrs Ramsden, of 25, Basil Mansions, Knightsbridge, SW3.

A Clerke of Oxenforde ...

From October 1940 to April 1941 Franklyn was living in Oxford. He had gone up to Exeter College, to read for a DPhil (though registered initially for a BLitt) under the supervision of AB Emden, Principal of St Edmund Hall.[58] This project came to a temporary end in 1941, because he returned to practising medicine on account of the war, but he never returned to Oxford to complete the work, even for a BLitt (though one does have to wonder how he would take even constructive criticism of his research).

It is probably fair to say that Oxford laid its glamour on Franklyn in a big way. Not only are his preferred robe and hood patterns mainly those of Oxford, but he went to extraordinary (and somewhat questionable) lengths to mark his rather slight connexion with the university. He appears in the University Calendar from 1941 until 1956 in both the Exeter and the general University lists, and in the University list only from 1956–65: from the 1966 volume he is not listed at all,[59] so to claim to be a 'Member' of the college as late as 1970, as he does on the title page Academical Dress, is decidedly exaggerating his connexion with the college: members of College ('Old Members' or 'Alumni'

---

[56] *Yorkshire Post and Leeds Gazette*, 9 December 1946. I am grateful to Dr Paul Coxon for bringing this to my attention. Was this the same family that set up the fish-and-chip empire?

[57] *Yorkshire Post and Leeds Gazette*, 28 February 1947.

[58] I am grateful to Ms Penelope Baker, Archivist of Exeter College, for information in this paragraph. The projected DPhil has not been known of before this, although he says in the Prologue to Academical Dress that he 'devoted one academic year, October 1940 to June 1941, to research in the Bodleian Library' – the two-month discrepancy is interesting. Alfred Brotherston Emden (1888–1979) was Principal of St Edmund Hall 1929–51. He was an historian of the mediæval Church, and is best-known for his two-volume *Biographical Register of Oxford to AD 1500*, and its sister volumes on Cambridge.

[59] I am grateful to Dr Alex Kerr, for this information.

are the current terms) are regarded as those who have attended the College and graduated with an Oxford degree.[60] His link with both Oxford University and Exeter College are thus tenuous at best. He also altered his entry in The Medical Directory. After the medic's various qualifications, the institutions where he or she trained are listed in italics in parentheses, before a list of posts held. Until the 1940 edition, Franklyn's entry read '(Univ. Lond. and Lausanne)'. From the 1941 edition, it reads '(St Thos & Univs Oxf, Lond, Laus)', which really is an outrageous piece of hubris, if not a downright lie, as of course Oxford had no part in his training.

It is not known what his thesis was to have been on: quite likely some aspect of academic dress, as he is noted as being 'interested in university history and protocol'.[61] Whether the project was not resumed because Norman Hargreaves-Mawdsley wrote his doctoral thesis on not only academic, but also legal, dress between 1955 and 1958 must remain a moot point. Hargreaves-Mawdsley graduated BA in 1948, and in 1955 commenced his research, submitting his thesis in 1958.[62] Is it possible that Franklyn's 1972 book *Academical Dress* is in fact the preparatory work for his thesis?

Hargreaves-Mawdsley's thesis is embargoed in perpetuity (it runs to 753 pages in three volumes), but the substance was published in 1963 in his two books on academic and legal dress up to 1800.[63] Franklyn is noted amongst those who have 'given me exceptional assistance' on page viii of the academic dress volume, where he also says he is 'especially indebted' to Emden, and so one assumes that Emden supervised Hargreaves-Mawdsley also. The dates fit so well that one is tempted to think that Hargreaves-Mawdsley's work brought Franklyn's own venture into academia to a halt. While he was at Oxford, Franklyn attempted to initiate a revision of the academic dress.[64]

Wickham Hill House

When he left Oxford, he settled at Wickham Hill House, Hassocks, in Sussex, where he was to remain almost until his death. This may well have been made possible by his mother's death. His father (the stockbroker) left only £5 893, but his mother, who died in 1937, left £20 129 – which may also have

---

[60] There is an argument for saying that anyone who has matriculated is and remains a member of a College, but even so, except for self-aggrandisement, it is hard to see why one would draw attention to a failed or abandoned enterprise of a few months in this way.

[61] As he was registered for the BLitt and had not been upgraded to the DPhil, the title of the thesis is not recorded, merely the field of interest.

[62] Alex Kerr, 'Hargreaves-Mawdsley's *History of Academical Dress* and the Pictorial Evidence for Great Britain and Ireland: Notes and Corrections', *Transactions of the Burgon Society* 8 (2008) 106–150, page 107.

[63] William N Hargreaves-Mawdsley, *A History of Academical Dress in Europe Until the End of the Eighteenth Century*, Oxford University Press (1963) and William N Hargreaves-Mawdsley, *A History of Legal Dress in Europe Until the End of the Eighteenth Century*, Oxford University Press (1963).

[64] See further, Chapter 5.

made the Oxford venture possible.[65] The house was not far from Lancing College, where George Shaw was on the staff from 1958. Wickham Hill is part of the B2116, the road which links Hurstpierpoint with Hassocks.

The end

Franklyn eventually became incapable of looking after himself, and was moved late in 1980 to a nursing home at 44 Sackville Gardens in Hove.[66] He later moved to Great Fish Hall in Tonbridge, which at that time was a nursing home (was the choice fortuitous, or was he deliberately returning to the town of his old school?),[67] and he died there on 26 November 1982, aged 86.[68] The causes of death were listed as 'a. Coronary Thrombosis; b. Hypertension', so his high blood pressure did eventually catch up with him: it cannot have been helped by his irascible temper. The death was registered by his niece, Margaret Ann Owens. His occupation is given as 'Medical Practitioner (retired)': one imagines a faint posthumous cry of '... a *physician*, not a medical practitioner!'.

The funeral was held at All Saints' Church, Putney, and he is buried in Putney Vale Cemetery, in his grandfather's grave.[69] Although he left a sum of money to his executors to maintain both that grave and that of his parents ('the continuance of the proper care of the Grave of my Parents in Charlton Park Cemetery and that of my Grandfather ... as I have done in my lifetime keeping the lettering thereon legible and causing the same to be recut and refilled when necessary for the purpose') and stating that they were to add 'a suitable inscription to my memory', he does not specify what the inscription is to say. Given his controlling nature, this is most interesting.

Afterword

Given Franklyn's obsession with status, it is worth noting that two of Henry Franklyn's descendants married into the aristocracy.

His daughter Violet Alice Maud (1866–1925) married Sir Humphrey de Trafford, baronet. Their son, Humphrey (1891–1971) married Cynthia, the grand-daughter of George Henry Cadogan, Earl Cadogan, and had four daughters,

---

[65] National Probate Calendar (Index of Wills and Administrations) 1858–1966, s.vv. Franklyn, Aubrey Hamilton, and Franklyn, Ethel Mary. The equivalent of £20 129 in 2013 would be £4 437 000.00 (economic status) or £1 133 000.00 (purchasing power). Information from http://www.measuringworth.com/ukcompare/relativevalue.php (accessed 13 May 2014). Assuming this was split equally between her three children, Franklyn was still very comfortably off.

[66] Casey, 'Academic Dress: Personal Reminiscences', page 153. The address is given in letters from Franklyn to Casey.

[67] William Franklyn and Hugh de Caustions held the eighth part of a knight's fee in the Manor of Caustions in the parish of Hadlow: Great Fish Hall is on the Hadlow Road.

[68] Death certificate.

[69] Will, page 2, Clause IV.

the eldest of whom, Anne (1918–87) married Derek Parker-Bowles, whose son Andrew was the first husband of Camilla Shand, now Queen Consort.

His grandson Henry Walter (1867–1915) married Edith Cecilia, daughter of Richard Curzon, Earl Howe.

Another grandson, George Frederick Edward Essex, married Mary Gertrude,[70] the widow of Charles Henry Lascelles. (It is not clear how he was related to the Earls of Harewood, but their only child, born in the USA, was called Gerald Harewood.)

---

[70] Franklyn in *SGH* gives her maiden name as 'Terry', no dates, and merely 'of USA'. She was in fact born in Yorkshire.

2 Franklyn's Character

It is for his highly abrasive character that Franklyn is remembered as much as for his achievements, and thus a chapter dedicated to this aspect of him is necessary: some idea of it has already been given in the previous chapter. Those who met him found him without exception 'difficult'. George Shaw recalled him as 'irascible and opinionated', which may well stand as an overall judgment – and may explain his underlying high blood-pressure problem.[1] As will become apparent, Franklyn was not backward in promoting his own opinions and achievements, nor in decrying those of others when they conflicted with his ideas – which was almost always. It becomes plain that he saw things very much in black and white, and that there was anything in between simply did not register with him.

There is a great deal we do not know about him, of course: what he liked to read, what music and radio stations he listened to, what TV programmes he watched (assuming he had a TV). None of this we can hope to recover. We do know he was devoted to a succession of cats; one might have thought a dog would have better fitted the persona he projected.

While he was living in Lincoln he appeared as a defendant in a civil case.[2] He had bought a car from the Alvis car company in Coventry in July 1937, for £850, with a one-year guarantee. In March 1939, Franklyn returned it to Alvis for repairs, as the silencing system had been damaged in use, and he was charged half price for a new one. In May new shock absorbers were fitted – initially at half price, but 'after a good deal of correspondence' (one can well imagine this), no charge was made. In September further work was done, for which he considered he had been overcharged, and finally in December he sent it back again for repairs, including demanding that a special painter be employed for the repainting of 'certain parts of the car'.[3] Eight men at once were occupied in dealing with the works, and the firm charged accordingly. He refused to pay, as he claimed that some of the work had not been carried out, and also that he had been charged for repairing a damaged bonnet, which

---

[1] George Shaw once asked Franklyn to dinner, and his wife prohibited him from ever doing so again.

[2] *The Coventry Standard*, 20 January 1940, page 2. The headline is 'Works on a Car: Coventry Firm's successful claim'.

[3] Is it going too far to think that this might be his armorial achievement on the doors?

damage he said was done by the firm's employees, in his presence and that of his chauffeur. The judge deducted this, but ordered him to pay £14 6s 6d in settlement.

A good deal of material – all confirmatory of this attitude – has been turned up in recent research on the robes in the universities for which he designed. In December 1953, BA Chalmers, the Registrar at the University of Southampton, wrote to the Registrar at the then University College, Hull:

> I can say unreservedly that he [Franklyn] is a man of un-
> doubted authority on the subject and that, in view of the com-
> plexity and profusion of academic plumage, we found it a great
> relief to have someone who could suggest an original and logi-
> cal system. He does not expect payment other than expenses
> although I gather he hopes to receive an honorary degree –
> not a Doctorate of course, a mastership is sufficient – for his
> services. He is, of course, an eccentric, completely absorbed
> in academic ceremonial and dress, and will try to take charge
> of your whole ceremonial arrangements in addition to making
> lengthy speeches at every opportunity on his dress propos-
> als. Unfortunately, he is so lacking in a sense of humour and
> so convinced of the supreme importance of being properly
> dressed – academically – that if one gives him too much rope,
> one is eventually faced with the necessity of being rather rude
> to him in order to get him under control. It is a great pity that
> this is so, because he can be extremely useful – however, if
> you are forewarned, as I was not, perhaps you can keep him
> in order from the beginning. I do not want you to think that
> I am attacking Franklyn – we think that what he produced
> was worth the trouble we had with him – but he is such an
> odd character that I felt duty bound to pass on what was our
> experience.[4]

This tendency is made plain in the unsolicited letter he sent to Hull offering to design their robes.[5] It contains a list of principles to be adhered to, and sets out in some detail the basics of a scheme (his usual one of a university silk lining with faculty borders) and its rationale: all this in an initial letter which merely indicated his interest. His inability to let minor matters go can be seen here – a literary counterpart of the 'lengthy speeches' referred to above:

> The arms of Kingston upon Hull (duly recorded in HM College
> of Arms) are blazoned: 'Azure, three ducal coronets or' ('in

[4] File of un-catalogued correspondence relating to the Academic Dress Committee (1953–55). Letter from Chalmers (University of Southampton) to Registrar. I am grateful to Dr Richard Baker for allowing me to reproduce this from his work on Hull.

[5] Letter, CAHF to the Registrar of Hull, 12 November 1953; quoted in: Richard Baker, 'The Academic Dress of the University of Hull from 1954 to the Present Day, Including the Hull–York Medical School from 2003', *Transactions of the Burgon Society* 11 (2011) 30–58, pages 30–31.

pale' is redundant, just as 'three leopards, passant guardant'
in the Royal Arms would naturally be placed one above the
other unless otherwise stated).[6]

Everything he has placed in parentheses could well have been omitted: one
feels he is blaming the University for what he saw as the incorrect blazon!
It also illustrates another side of him: behaving as if a suggestion was fact.
When he wrote to Hull, the charter had not been granted, but he behaved as
if it had. This appears in his attempt to reform Oxford's dress in 1941 (see
page 69): he suggested a committee be set up to undertake the task, and then
behaved as if it had been, while the reality was that the University had not
decided whether to do so.

Ten years later, Franklyn wrote to the authorities at the nascent University of
Warwick offering to design a system of robes. The Vice-Chancellor designate,
Jack Butterworth, contacted John Brooke-Little, then Bluemantle Pursuivant
at the College of Arms, to ask about Franklyn. Brooke-Little replied that

> Dr Charles Franklin [sic] is well known at the College of Arms
> and I am quite certain that he is competent to design academic
> dress. I think I should perhaps warn you in confidence that
> he is an extremely difficult character to deal with, however, I
> have no doubt that you will discover this for yourself in due
> course.[7]

Franklyn was quite insistent in his attempt to get appointed at Warwick,
and wrote several times, trumpeting his own achievements. A serene self-
assurance of his gaining the appointment appears in a letter of 9 December
1963:

> I do not mind how many others have approached the V-C,
> as my position is unique ... for no other living individual has
> designed the complete system of academical & official dress for
> 4 British universities, has made a speciality of the subject for
> 53 years (1910–63), has been responsible for the long article in
> 'The Encyclopædia Britannica' since June 1941, in 'Chambers'
> Encyclopædia' since Dec. 1961 (new edition in press soon) &
> has read a paper on the subject before the Oxf. Univ. Arch.
> Soc.[8]

The Vice-Chancellor of Warwick finally contacted his opposite number at
Southampton, who advised him that 'he turned out to be a person whom

---

[6] Ibid. He was, of course, wrong: 'Where three similar charges are placed on a shield it is assumed
that two are in chief and one in base, *unless otherwise specified*': S Friar, ed., *A New Dictionary
of Heraldry*, Alphabooks/A&C Black (1987), pages 61–62. (My emphases.)

[7] Quoted in: Jackson, 'The Development of Academic Dress in the University of Warwick',
page 13. Brooke-Little spelt the name with an -i-, possibly to make a point. The phrase 'well
known at the College of Arms', probably disguises a good deal of irritation with him.

[8] Quoted in: ibid., page 15. Again, note the unnecessary statements of details. Is he counting
Malaya and the ANU as 'British'? It is hard to see how otherwise the total of four can be arrived
at – unless he is counting the bogus universities.

it was not easy to work with, and I do not think therefore that I should encourage you to employ him', which is a step away from what Southampton had told Hull a decade earlier.[9]

This assessment of his own worth may be compared with one of nine years earlier. Obviously somewhat annoyed that Ede & Ravenscroft as well as Wippell (always Franklyn's preferred choice – 'the best robemaker in the country') were also being consulted at Hull, Franklyn responded to the Vice-Chancellor on the 13 December 1954:

> I feel rather concerned and have had something of a shock. It is probable that this will be my last University as with a sword hanging over my head, I cannot expect to live long enough to see another University created in England.[10] If July 19th were to be the crowning glory of a 45 years study, it would be wonderful but to fail in 1955 would be utter devastation and to be rejected (after the system had been supposed to be accepted) would indeed be mortifying. If the subject had not been the passion of my life since 1910 I should feel, quite naturally, far less acutely about it.
>
> With all due respects John F Austin is a tailor: I am a University graduate and in point of fact, a graduate of three universities.[11] He joined Ede & R. only recently, after the war, from another type of business.[12]

'Austin' was Col John F Austin, MVO, who was Managing Director of Ede & Ravenscroft. He was an authority on academic dress and had a reputation for insisting on very precise and specific colour shades, and was entrusted with specific responsibilities for the ceremonial robes at the 1953 Coronation.[13] 'A tailor', indeed. An unlooked-for result of Franklyn's insisting on using Wippell was that Hull also obtained quotes from Ede & Ravenscroft, and they were awarded the contract: 'I do hope our somewhat eccentric friend has not queered the pitch' wrote Wood of Hull to Wippell[14] – but he had.

Much the same was the case at Essex (founded 1964), where he was particularly incensed at not obtaining the task of designing the robes – see

---

[9] Quoted in: Jackson, 'The Development of Academic Dress in the University of Warwick', page 15.

[10] It is unclear what this 'sword' was: probably his high blood pressure, and consequent fear of a stroke. In the event, he was to see the foundation of twenty-four new universities in the 1960s, as well as the CNAA, the Open University, and University College, Buckingham, as he had another twenty-eight years left. It was his last scheme, however, as of those twenty-four only the New University of Ulster had any input from him – and that was merely the principles, rather than a complete scheme.

[11] London, Lausanne, and Malaya – the last *hon caus*.

[12] File of un-catalogued correspondence relating to the Academic Dress Committee (1953-1955). Letter from Franklyn to the Vice-Chancellor 13 December 1954.

[13] Personal communication, the Revd Philip Goff.

[14] Wippell's file relating to the University of Hull (1953-1955). Letter from Wood Brothers of Hull to Knott, 7 September 1954. Wood Bros were the local outfitters, who supplied the robes.

pages 77–80.[15]

It is highly likely that similar correspondences from Franklyn exist in the archives of the other universities created in the 1960s. In particular, we await research into his two other schemes, Southampton and Ulster.

The dedication to *Academical Dress* (page iii) repays study. The book is dedicated to 'the Universities of Oxford, Cambridge, Lausanne, London, Malaya (Singapore), Southampton, Hull, the Australian National University, and Tonbridge School'. It then goes on to mention Lynne Rosemary Marlow, SRN,

> whose character, charm, comeliness, kindness, personality, sweet nature, devotion to duty, and essential goodness were a constant encouragement, and made her the brightest star in the firmament.

The words 'Annie Zunz' – 11–22 August 1969' then appear. Annie Zunz (neé Bartlett) was the Irish wife of a German iron merchant, Siegfried Rudolf Zunz, who had come to London from Frankfurt-am-Main in 1860 to make his fortune. The couple were married for 22 years, but were childless, and when Annie died in 1896 her husband was inconsolable. He decided that after his death (which happened three years after his wife's) that his fortune was to be used to perpetuate her memory. In his will he instructed his executors and trustees to give £25 000 (about £1.9 million today) to 'a London hospital' to build and maintain forever a ward named 'The Annie Zunz ward'. The hospital chosen turned out to be St Mary's Hospital, Paddington, but the estate also made payments to other London hospitals, and so Annie Zunz wards can be found at Great Ormond Street, The Royal Free, St Bartholomew's, King's College Hospital, the Bolingbroke, the Chelsea and Westminster, and the Royal London.[16] These wards specialize in a variety of fields: gynæcology; endocrinology; elderly care. Franklyn spent eleven days in 1969 on the Annie Zunz Ward at the Westminster.[17] It is not clear what the Annie Zunz Ward there specialized in, but as he was then seventy-three, it was possibly some geriatric problem, or maybe some recurrence of the 'sword hanging over my head' referred to in his letter to the Vice-Chancellor of Hull in 1954.[18] But clearly the irascible Franklyn, as so many other such difficult men, was won over by this female member of the nursing staff, and his sentimental side appears. What possible interest she may have had in the topic of academic dress is unknown, but as the Prologue is dated 21 June 1969, and the publication date on page i is June 1970, it could be that Franklyn was indeed

---

[15] I am very grateful to the Revd Edmund Eggleston for passing me copies of the Franklyn correspondence in the Essex archive.

[16] Information from http://hharp.org/library/gosh/general/ward-names.html (accessed 27 April 2014).

[17] He does not specify in the dedication, but the in list of subscribers to *Academical Dress* lists Miss Marlow at both her home address and at The Westminster Hospital. Her copy was 'presented by the author'.

[18] See page 18 *supra*.

seriously ill (or thought he was), and maybe despaired of seeing the book through the press.[19]

Under Miss Marlow's name is a line in parentheses: ('Rodelinda': clear light blue eyes) On the surface, this appears to be innocuous, but when we come to deal with his will, we see that Franklyn was in fact obsessed with such things. He refers to his grand-niece Phillipa Anne Irene as 'the blue-eyed fair-haired only daughter ...', and goes on to 'express the devout hope that the man whom she marries eventually will have blue eyes so that she does not mix the races and that the next generation may be Saxons pure-blooded, blue-eyed, fair haired, as she is herself'. This is also overtly expressed in his initial letter to the University of Hull, putting himself forward to design their robes:

> We should also bear in mind those fair-haired, as well as red-haired, blue-eyed Scandinavian people of the sea, from Norway, Sweden, Jutland, and Saxony, who landed on our east coast in waves and waves until our English blood was (at one time) 75% Scandinavian (the Master Race and nature's masterpiece).[20]

Research reveals that Franklyn was a member of the committee of the Racial Preservation Society, founded in June 1965 by Robin Beauclaire and James Doyle.[21] It advocated 'the Christian Response to the Racial Problem'. The Society apparently functioned as a propaganda group without branching into politics (although individual members were free to join political parties) and provided extensive lists of conspiratorial books and pamphlets for sale. It was prosecuted under the Race Relations Act in 1968 at Lewes Crown Court for incitement to racial hatred by distributing pamphlets: five members were indicted, but the case was dismissed, owing to the careful way in which the relevant pamphlets had been phrased. It was amalgamated with the British National Party (BNP) and the League of Empire Loyalists in the National Front when it was inaugurated in 1967.[22] It is unclear how extensive Franklyn's later involvement with this was. See his views as expressed in his will, page 115.

Rodelinda, on the other hand, is the title of an opera of 1725 by Handel

---

[19] A search on Ancestry.com suggests a Lynne Rosemary Marlow who was born in Fulham in 1948, and married Robert Horrobin in 1974.

[20] Letter, CAHF to the Registrar of Hull, 12 November 1953 (quoted in: Baker, 'The Academic Dress of the University of Hull', pages 31–32). If nothing else, it reveals a shocking lack of grasp of genetics and early mediæval history.

[21] *The Institute of Race Relations Newsletter*, December 1967, page 9. The committee was: James Doyle (chairman), Raymond Bamford, MA (vice-chairman), J Wilkinson (treasurer), John Grenville Stuart (secretary), the Revd Stephen E Pulford, Dr Charles Franklyn, the Revd H Nicholson, Dr David Brown, T Hall, and Mrs D Hardy.

[22] See further the Wikipedia article on the Racial Preservation Society, at https://en.wikipedia.org/wiki/Racial_Preservation_Society (accessed 6 January 2020). See also: W Laverick and P Joyce, *Racial and Religious Hate Crime: The UK From 1945 to Brexit*, Palgrave Macmillan (2019), page 68ff.

(*Rodelinda, regina de' Longobardi*). The significance of this is unclear, and has probably gone to the grave with Franklyn, though the Langobards/Lombards were a Germanic people, and possibly he regarded them as being fair-haired and blue-eyed: we may, perhaps, therefore assume that Miss Marlow was, besides blue-eyed, fair-haired.

Personal interactions with Franklyn by various academic dress afficionados were very varied. Arthur Casey went to visit Franklyn several times, and found him to be contrary.[23] The first visit resulted in a lecture on the dangers of salt in the diet; on another, when he asked Franklyn about the origins of the DMus cream damask robes, he was given a disquisition on Haydn being the greatest composer: in both cases almost wilfully refusing to discuss the matter of common interest. After Franklyn's death, he wrote to the family to ask if he might buy any of Franklyn's books on academic dress.

> To my surprise, I had a very rude letter by return of post from a man who accused me of harassing his wife. I wrote back immediately saying that my intentions had been completely misunderstood. I soon had a letter from their solicitor threatening action if I did not stop writing to them.[24]

This was Franklyn's sister, Irene, and her husband, Theobald Owens; their younger brother, Harold, had also died in 1982. It would seem that the abrasive nature may have been a family trait.

On the other hand, Professor Len Newton also went to see him, and managed to get pictures of Franklyn wearing various robes, and found him to be very charming.[25] Is this the difference between an accredited academic and one of what Daisy Ashford called the 'mere people'?[26]

John Balsdon went to see Franklyn three times. The first was to consult him as a blood-pressure specialist ('Avoid bread: it is the work of the devil. It has too much salt in it'). He took his Sussex bachelor's robes to show, and Franklyn was suitably disparaging of them. Franklyn asked him to return, bringing a friend, who had to be quite tall, so that they could photograph his hoods, which duly happened. Franklyn then asked him to visit a third time, so that John could take him to Parham House: 'I need to educate you about heraldry'. He was duly led round the house, portrait by portrait, while Franklyn held forth at great length on the heraldry in each, in a loud voice, and took particular delight in doing so if a tour guide was attempting to address a group nearby, talking over them, and explaining why they were (in his opinion) wrong. John decided that he would not visit again.[27]

---

[23] Casey, 'Academic Dress: Personal Reminiscences', pages 152–153.
[24] Ibid., pages 152–153.
[25] These pictures are, so far as is known, the only ones in existence of CAHF in academic dress, other than the back view with the 'four most beautiful and dignified hoods in the world' which forms the famous frontispiece to the 1972 edition of *Degrees and Hoods*.
[26] Daisy Ashford, *The Young Visiters*, Chatto & Windus (1919), Chapter 6: '... tall Life Guards keeping off the mere people who had gathered to watch the nobility clatter up.'
[27] John Balsdon, personal communication.

It is quite clear that Franklyn was a very controlling person. This is evident in the utterly unworkable stipulation in the front of the two large works on academic dress – *Academical Dress* and the fifth edition of *Degrees and Hoods* – that each successive owner of a copy must write to Franklyn, that Cambridge University Library will keep a record of all copies, and that he will 'buy back at once any copy that gets onto to the market'.[28] Quite how all this was supposed to work once he died is unclear. But it is very clear that he wished to control who had access to these books. Arthur Casey wrote in 1980 to see if he could buy a copy of *Degrees and Hoods* and received a reply on 25 February 1980.[29] It starts by noting that Casey's letter had arrived 'at 7.50 today'. He provided the name of a person in Oxford who he thought had a copy for sale, and asks that if Arthur was 'lucky and got it' then would he let Franklyn know. There is then an odd little sentence: 'What about my postage, please?'

Another letter was written on 11 March, for which Franklyn used as notepaper a white envelope which had been sent him by the Wellcome Foundation. He left the address label on, and wrote 'From' beside it. It was addressed to Charles AH Franklyn, Esq, MD', and Franklyn then added after the MD '(Physician)'. (See Figure 1.)[30] The letter is exceptionally difficult to decipher, but it starts out by acknowledging receipt of one of 8th March 'at 11.15 today', and immediately says 'Please CONFIRM that you have purchased' the book, and that on the back of the title page has been added 'Purchased on 8/3/80 from ...' and the seller's name follows. It was to be signed by Casey now that he owned the copy. The anxiety that Franklyn was not able to control this transaction and that a copy might 'go feral' is tangible.

There are two further letters to Arthur, dating from October 1980, by which time Franklyn was living at Sackville Gardens. The first, dated 8 October, follows up a visit that Arthur had made to him, and enquires about Dr Mawdsley's copy of *Academical Dress* – this is Hargreaves-Mawdsley.[31] It ends, 'Please remember to send my stamps'. The envelope is reused, with stamp-paper stuck over the original address, the original postmark being Dumbarton. The stamp is a Scottish 10p one: did he reuse that too, as it bears no earlier franking? There is also a PS scrawled on the flap of it: 'What date did Mawdsley die?' The final letter, dated 28 October, opens 'You sent NO stamps, so I have had to stick 2 from another man. Please send them to me.' He then goes on to upbraid Arthur: 'You have not answered my important question, i.e., what became of Dr Mawdsley's copy' of *Academical Dress*. 'Has his widow got it? or is it in Canada? You must know!'. The envelope is again reused with stamp-paper stuck over the original address, but there is

---

[28] Apparently CUL has no knowledge of this, and has no such list (personal communication, Dr Paul Coxon).

[29] Letter, CAHF to Casey, 25 February 1980. I am grateful to Mr Casey for providing copies of this and three other letters from Franklyn.

[30] Another such letter exists – written to the Chief Clerk of the University of Durham.

[31] Doubtless there is some complicated reason why Franklyn did not use the double-barrelled version of the name.

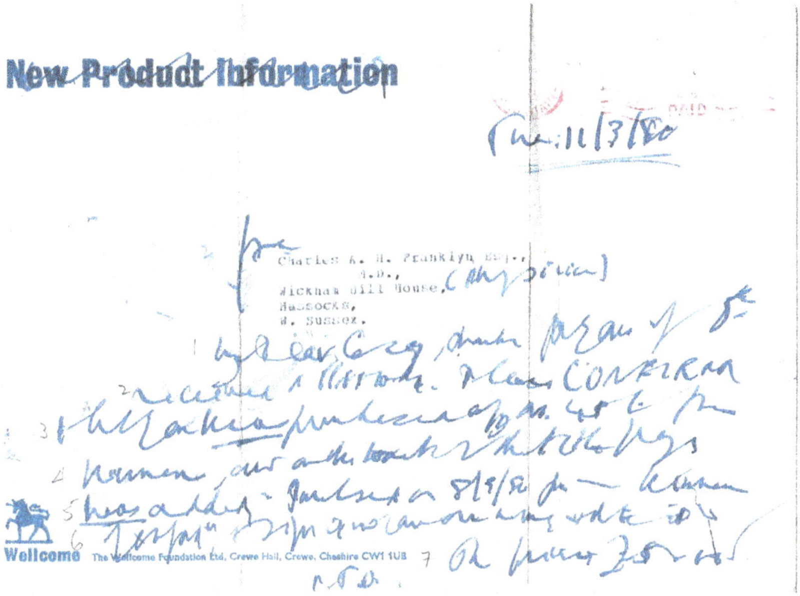

Figure 1: Letter to Arthur Casey, 11 March 1980

only one stamp (so where is the other?) and one postmark – Sussex Coast. The obsession with the minor expenditure of a stamp (it appears from the final letter that a first-class stamp in 1980 cost 12p) is quite extraordinary. Did he expect every correspondent to pay the postage both ways?

He also made similar stipulations in his will, attempting to control minutely the way his estate was to be administered for many years after his death.

There are various other sidelights on his character. One is that he was disinclined to put himself out in any way. In a letter to DJ Wallace of the Senate Department at the University of London, he says he will bring the University's copy of *Academical Dress* into London, but that if no-one could meet him to collect it, and he had to deliver himself, then it would 'cause loss of time, trouble, and delay'.[32]

In 1953, he was invited to attend a dinner at the University of Hull at which the guest of honour was to be Princess Mary, the Princess Royal. He assumed that academic dress would be worn, but was told that full evening dress was the order. He declined to attend:

> Had the reception and Dinner been a brilliant pageant of colour, a grand Academic occasion, I should have enjoyed it. I am deeply disappointed that it is ... a non-academic affair.

---

[32] Letter, CAHF to Wallace, 12 August 1970; BS Archive U/LOND/1/1/7. It is not clear where he was to be met: presumably delivery would have been to Senate House – a place he visited often, one assumes, as a leading light in Convocation!

Even a dinner-jacket would mean a third suitcase.[33]

There is a quite extraordinary letter from 1954, when he was travelling to Hull for a meeting about their academic dress:

> I shall travel up on the 3.50 p.m. from King's Cross, due at Hull at 8.59 p.m., take my room, go to bed at 9 p.m., and be cool, calm and collected on Tuesday.[34]

As has been remarked, quite how even Franklyn was to get from the station to the hotel, take his room, and be in bed all within one minute defies logic! The hotel was the Royal Station Hotel, which is situated above the station, and he demanded the same room (no 155) each time he stayed there. 'Cool, calm, and collected' is not a state of mind one associates with him.

On the other hand, he could make life exceptionally difficult for himself, although that stems from his controlling nature. This is best illustrated with the mailing of *Academical Dress*. Each copy had to be 'inscribed' – which he did with a blue ballpoint pen – and then sent out. What he seems to have done is to have bought a limited number of boxes (if not, indeed, just one) in which the books were sent to the subscribers, who then had to return the box and the string, together with stamps to the value of the postage, so that it could be used over and over again:

> Please be so good as to send as soon as possible a crossed cheque for £5.0.0. (sterling) crossed 'Book A/c'. The printers have to be paid an immense sum and this cannot be paid until the Author has received payment.[35]

> Please examine the stamps on the parcel and send stamps to the same value NOT added to the cheque: these are required urgently for other parcels waiting in the hall to go, and failure to do so holds up other subscribers who are waiting for their copies.

> Please return at once the precious BOX, string, and all wrappings, as the writer is a physician and does not run a box factory.[36]

As he remarked to Francis Steer:

> There are some 160 [altered to 206] copies to inscribe, number, date, sign, wrap, pack and post, which immense task will take me approximately 3 months: they will be despatched as quickly

---

[33]Letter, CAHF to the Registrar of Hull, 11 July 1953, quoted in: Baker, 'The Academic Dress of the University of Hull', page 42. One wonders what was in the other two suitcases – and why bringing his academic dress would not require a third suitcase. And if 'even' a dinner-jacket required a third, would tails require a fourth?

[34]Letter, CAHF to Wippell, 18 June 1954, quoted in: ibid., page 34.

[35]The immense sum was £1500 (letter from CAHF to Arthur Casey, 25 February 1980). This would be about £20 000 today, which does seem excessive for 500 books. The £5.00 purchase price is about £60.00 in 2020 values.

[36]Duplicated letter sent out with copies of *Academical Dress*.

as it is possible to do so.[37]

Why he did not require the buyers to add the cost of post and packing is beyond understanding, but he appears to have gone through the same rigmarole with *Degrees and Hoods* two years later.

A complicated character, and fertile ground for a psychological study. He was of almost the last generation which blocked their emotions in public, and to which one's exact social standing was very important, but whether his contemporaries were quite so prickly about such matters is difficult to say: possibly those who were born on the cusp of two social classes always were: can we see a sense of inferiority? But this does seem to have twisted his outlook. The serene self-assurance in his own accuracy which comes over again and again, and his obsession with detail, may perhaps hint at some form of autism or OCD. We cannot know, but we can wonder if, had he been born at a later time, when such things were less important, whether he would have turned out the same.

Possibly John Fowles pinned it down in *The French Lieutenant's Woman*:

> In London the beginnings of a plutocratic stratification of society had, by the mid-century [i.e., 1850] begun. Nothing of course took the place of good blood; but it had become generally accepted that good money and good brains could produce artificially a passable enough facsimile of acceptable social standing. Disraeli was the type, not the exception, of his times.[38]

We can, of course, see the early stirrings of this in Jane Austen's novels. It seems likely that Charles Franklyn, born in 1896, found himself in the full flood of that change as it eddied out from London, and, while it was money and brains that had enabled his family to attain its social position, he was attempting (as so many others did) to hide – or at least gloss over – the fact, and was pretending to 'good blood'.

---

[37] Letter, CAHF to Francis Steer, 7 January 1971.
[38] John Fowles, *The French Lieutenant's Woman*, Jonathan Cape, London (1969). The passage occurs towards the end of chapter 11.

3 Academic Awards

In addition to his MB,BS(Lond) and his MRCS and LRCP, Franklyn acquired a number of other distinctions, of varying degrees of credibility.

His entry in the *Medical Directory* for 1930 is a useful place to start. With abbreviations silently expanded, it reads:

> MD(Lausanne) 1925; MB,BS(Lond) (distinction in Physiology 2nd MB Pt II) 1924; MRCS(Eng), LRCP Lond 1923; MA Illinois, 1924; BSc 1921. Sutton Sams Prize in Midwifery St Thomas Hospital 1922–23; FSAScot; Member Standing Committee University of London Faculty of Medicine; Honorary Secretary Lausanne Medical Graduates Association & University of London Medical Graduates' Society; Fellow of the Royal Society of Medicine; Honorary Treasurer Bromley Medical Society; late Registrar, Cas, Officer & Out-patient Anæsthetist Victoria Hospital for Children, Chelsea; Clinical Assistant Children, Skin, Mental, and X-Ray Departments St Thomas Hospital, & Chelsea Hospital for Women; Research Student, Clinique Médicale, Cantonal Hospital University of Lausanne. Author 'Recherches cliniques sur la Pneumonie' Thèse, 1925; 'Bearing of Coat-Armour by Ladies' (illust) 1923; 'Nature & Uses of Refractometric & Viscosimetric Tests', *British Medical Journal*, 1926; 'History of the Family of Tiarks of Foxbury', 1925.[1]

University of Lausanne

As has been seen, he gained his MD at Lausanne, which appears to have been granted on the basis of an examination for which little extra work beyond his MB was required, and for which he produced a thesis on Pneumonia. His choice of Lausanne rather than the more obvious London would appear to be

---

[1] In the same year, his entry in *Kelly's Directory* for Kent gives 'MD, BS Lond, MRSC Eng, LRCP Lond, MA, FSA': was it deliberate that 'Lausanne' was omitted after the MD (thus implying it is a London degree), and 'Scot' after the FSA? The MA (unattributed) is the Lincoln-Jefferson; the BSc is not listed. In that for Bromley, etc, he listed 'MD Lausanne, MB,BS Lond, MRSC Eng, LRCP Lond'. The wide difference in three works of reference published in the same year is fascinating.

explained in *Academical Dress*, on page 211. Under the entry for Bruxelles, he remarks:

> The absurd and farcical situation which exists in Great Britain, where so many colleges, societies and licensing bodies grant registrable qualifications to practise medicine, such as MRCS, MRCP, LRCS, LRCP, LRFPS, – LSA, – LMSSA, – LAH, etc, which Diplomas do not grant or bestow the title of 'Doctor' nor the letters MD, has always been a source of bitter resentment and grievance to the majority of the medical practitioners in this country, and this led some of them to go abroad to obtain the letters, style and title of Doctor in Medicine, which their own country would not, and still will not, give them, under reasonable conditions. From about 1880–1920 the University of Brussels was willing to bestow this degree upon any duly registered practitioner after a special examination.[2]

The Bruxelles examination was, he says, discontinued 'after the Great War (a lamentable fact)'. Holders of British medical qualifications were admitted 'without further curriculum' to the examination – i.e., their knowledge was already sufficient to pass the degree.[3] It was made up of three parts, each of which had to be passed before attempting the next: the 'First Doctorate' involved examination in Medicine, Pathology, Therapeutics, Mental Diseases, and Diseases of Women and Children; the 'Second Doctorate', examinations in Surgery, Midwifery, Hygiene, and Medical Jurisprudence; and the 'Third Doctorate', clinical examinations in Medicine and Surgery, in Midwifery ('with the *mannequin*'), Ophthalmology, Operative Surgery, and Regional Anatomy with Dissections. The examination was held five times a year, and 'may be got through in about a week, and seldom exceeds eight to ten days'. Special importance was attached to practical knowledge. There was an Association of British Graduates of the Brussels University.[4] Academic robes were designed for use by its members: a robe of Cambridge pattern [d1], in scarlet, lined and faced with light blue silk, and a hood of London shape [f3], in scarlet lined light blue. It is not known who designed these robes, nor when they were designed.

Franklyn then says, under the entry for Lausanne, that during the last fifty years 'increasing numbers of British and other practitioners from overseas have been going to Swiss universities for an MD degree'.[5] Details of exactly what was required at Lausanne are not available, but it sounds as though the Lausanne degree also was conferred after an examination alone, and not

---

[2] Charles A H Franklyn, *Academical Dress from the Middle Ages to the Present Day, including Lambeth Degrees*, W E Baxter Ltd, Lewes, Sussex (1970), page 211. The inconsistent punctuation is intriguing. Was any kind of proof-reading undertaken?
[3] 'Degrees for Practitioners', *British Medical Journal* (31 August 1901) 556.
[4] Ibid.
[5] There was a long tradition before this of medics taking degrees from universities in other European countries: Leiden being one such in the eighteenth century.

after any further study.[6]

However, the MD at English universities, and London in particular, has always been available to any MB who has undertaken further work *at doctoral level* (which would appear to be 'reasonable conditions'), and there is no reason why Franklyn could not have gained the MD of London. The London MD in 1925 seems, like the Lausanne MD, to have consisted of an advanced examination: the submission of a thesis appears to have been the method least used. The University Calendar for 1924–25 states:

> The MD degree may be taken in any of the following branches, medicine, pathology, physiological medicine, midwifery and diseases of women, state medicine, tropical medicine. The examination is held twice annually. A thesis may be submitted, except in State Medicine'.[7]

So, unlike the Bruxelles MD, which required fourteen topics, the London MD required just one: it would be enlightening to know what Lausanne required. In 1924, twenty candidates took the London degree, four of whom were external students. At all universities, the MD has always been less demanding than the other higher doctorates (DD, LL.D, etc), being 'somewhat on the level of a PhD'.[8] Possibly part of the problem for Franklyn was that London required one to wait for four years after becoming MB,BS before submitting for the MD examination, whereas he gained the Lausanne degree within two years. Also, if the Lausanne degree, like the Bruxelles one, preferred practical over academic knowledge, this may tell us more about his academic ability, especially if London's advanced examination was a written one.

What Franklyn seems to be saying, and actually says in as many words elsewhere, is that the MB is the equivalent of a doctoral degree, and should be so treated in terms of its academic dress: '... consequently, a special hood should have been awarded always to these special, almost doctor, degrees';[9] but he stops short of advocating the American practice of granting the MD as a first degree.[10] He seems unable (or unwilling?) to understand that the length of a course has nothing to do with the level at which it is assessed. (Current practice regards the MB as the equivalent of a taught master's degree, on a level with MSc, etc.)

---

[6]This is no longer the case. Though Lausanne still welcomes foreign students, the medical doctorate is now called a 'Doctorate in Medicine and in Sciences, MD-PhD' and requires a good deal of work at doctoral level. <http://www.unil.ch/mdphd> (accessed 27 April 2014). Correspondence with the University reveals that they no longer hold any records of the earlier MD examination, nor of those who took it.

[7]London University Calendar for 1924–5. I am grateful to Dr Paul Coxon for this information.

[8]R Stevens, *Medical Practice in Modern England: The Impact of Specialization and State Medicine*, Yale University Press (2003), page 21. Indeed, it is now ranked with the professional doctors (EngD, EdD, etc) at most universities.

[9]Franklyn, *Academical Dress*, page 199.

[10]Apparently adopted in the eighteenth century from contemporary Scottish practice: the Scottish MB was a nineteenth-century introduction. Columbia was the first American university to award an MD.

And yet. At this time, the MB(Cantab) was wearing a hood of black silk lined mid-cherry silk; the MChir had black silk lined scarlet silk. This was altered in the 1934 revision,[11] when the black and mid-cherry hood went to the MChir, and the MB got mid-cherry and fur. However, the MB gown, if correctly made, is the doctoral dress robe in black stuff, but without coloured sleeve-linings and facings. These MB robes had come into being in the mid-1880s.[12] Franklyn, in *Academical Dress*, page 185, notes that, for economy, robemakers were merely looping the sleeves of the BA gown (made without the slit), and not making the MB gown correctly. However, it this abbreviated form that has now, since the 1934 reforms, become the correct one for the MB gown, and those based on it. Thus the Cambridge MB in 1925 was arrayed in quasi-doctoral robes, merely replacing black for scarlet, and omitting the facings and sleeve-linings on the gown. As will become apparent, his ignorance (wilful or otherwise) of aspects of the history and development of academic dress is astonishing for one who set himself up as the sole expert in the land.

He was also highly disparaging of degrees in Surgery, and it is noteworthy that as a rule he dropped his BS from his list of post-nominals fairly early on – although London always addressed him as 'MD, BS'. So far as Oxford was concerned, he thought the MCh was the equivalent of a doctorate, and should be given doctoral-style robes, but in black rather than scarlet;[13] he appears unaware of the BCh. At Cambridge, he was annoyed by the BChir[14] hood – which was the MB hood less the fur on the cape. 'Luckily, the ridiculous and always crazy BCh degree has now been virtually abolished ... as in the Spring of 1937 the granting of the BCh alone was cancelled'.[15]

University of Malaya

The University of Malaya gave him an MA *hon: caus:* when he designed their robes in 1949.

Other 'degrees'

Among the degrees listed in the *Medical Directory* are an MA and a BSc. The BSc was taken in 1921, while he was an undergraduate at St Thomas, and the MA in 1924 when he graduated MB,BS of London. They are designated (Ill), which is is 'Illinois'. This is not the University of Illinois, but a common piece

---

[11] Into which, as we shall see, Franklyn had a great input.
[12] See: Nicholas Groves, 'The Academic Robes of Graduates of the University of Cambridge from the End of the Eighteenth Century to the Present Day', *Transactions of the Burgon Society* 13 (2013) 74–100. It is unclear why the MB hood had no fur; possibly on the model of the BD.
[13] Franklyn, *Academical Dress*, page 169.
[14] He invariably refers to BCh and MCh, not BChir and MChir, which is Cambridge's use.
[15] It is now awarded *in absentia* to all medical graduates when the exam results are published, and they receive the MB at the graduation ceremony, so they appear in the BChir robes.

of misdirection. These worthless 'degrees' were conferred by the 'Lincoln-Jefferson University' (LJU), 'a diploma-mill operated for several years in Chicago and northern Indiana'.[16] It was founded in 1897 by two Episcopalian clergymen, F J B Walker and Arthur Worger-Slade.[17] They were caught out by the American Medical Association when selling medical degrees in Japan and India.[18] LJU was chartered in the state of Illinois, which, according to an article in the *Sheffield Daily Telegraph*, was 'a conspicuous offender' in the granting of charters to all manner of so-called educational institutions.[19]

The use of the place of charter rather than the institution's name directs attention away from the worthlessness of the 'degree'.[20] LJU was attacked in the press, and one really has to wonder why Franklyn took these worthless 'degrees' in the first place, and then listed them in a professional directory, and why he carried on doing so as late as 1942 at least, well after LJU had been convicted of selling fraudulent medical degrees.[21] The identification is made secure by the picture of one of Franklyn's hoods taken by John Balsdon. This is of the 'improved' Burgon shape, in black, lined purple, with a wide white chevron, and the cowl edge bound 1" white (see Figure 2). He told John Balsdon that it was 'some American university', but not which. LJU is listed in the first three editions of Haycraft (1923, 1924, and 1927), but not in the 1947 one. It appears twice: once under the standard Intercollegiate Code listings, where the lining is indeed given as purple, with a white chevron – and it is noted as a 'wide chevron' in the 1927 edition. But there is also a listing under the non-ICC universities, where the hoods are said to be of 'full shape, with rounded corners'. The MA is given as 'black silk, lined purple silk, edged 1 inch white silk', and the BSc as 'purple stuff lined white silk, edged 1 inch old gold silk'.[22] So what Franklyn had was an amalgam of the two designs, with the alteration of the expected ICC simple shape to Burgon. And although he had spent several minutes fussing around to get it arranged as he wished, it is clearly on backwards.

These 'degrees' do not appear in his own entry in the Short Genealogical

---

[16] *Degree-conferring Institutions: Hearings before the Sub-committee on Judiciary of the Committee on the District of Columbia House of Representatives; seventh congress, first session, on HR 7951, March 23, 24, April 2, 3, and 5, 1928*, Government Printing Office, Washington (1928), page 65.

[17] Walker went to Medicine Hat, Canada, in 1926 and Slade came to England in 1927, where he had permission to officiate at Coggeshall in Essex, and then held a living in the Diocese of Worcester. (Worger would appear to have been his middle name, which he hyphenated to his surname: this is how he is listed in *Crockford's*.)

[18] *Degree-conferring Institutions*, page 66, quoting from the *Saturday Night* of Toronto, 23 April 1927.

[19] *Sheffield Daily Telegraph*, 8 June 1922, page 2.

[20] Graduates of the now-defunct 'Knightsbridge University' frequently put (as it might be) PhD(Denmark) after their names, the institution being chartered there – there being, of course, no such thing as the University of Denmark.

[21] 1942 is the latest edition of the *Medical Directory* I have been able to consult. He also listed the MA in the Tonbridge School Register.

[22] Frank W Haycraft, *The Degrees and Hoods of the World's Universities & Colleges*, third edition, The Cheshunt Press, London and Cheshunt (1927), page 69.

Figure 2: John Balsdon wearing Franklyn's MA hood from Lincoln-Jefferson University

History.[23]

Following Franklyn's listing in the Medical Directory, a second MA is listed from 1949 – MA(Intercoll) honoris causa. This was the 'Intercollegiate University', another notorious degree-mill. Founded as the College of Church Musicians in 1888 in association with the American Catholic Church,[24] and chartered in Kansas, it later added 'Intercollegiate University' to its name.[25] An English branch was established by John Churchill Sibley, a bishop within that denomination.[26] Despite an annual service at St George Bloomsbury, after which honorary degrees were handed out, it was excoriated in the press, and Sibley characterized as 'the Most Rev Dr Bunkum, a dealer in bogus degrees'.[27] It did not follow the Intercollegiate Code, but had a hood system of its own, and is duly listed in the first three Haycrafts. In 1938, the hoods were revised, and this new scheme has all the marks of Franklyn on it (see further, pages 54–55), so it would seem likely that he was granted an MA for this work. Again, one wonders quite how he justified listing the award. The Intercollegiate was closed in 1942, and succeeded by 'the University of

---

[23]Franklyn, *SGH*.

[24]An independent body, not the American branch of the Roman Catholic Church.

[25]*Truth*, 24 October 1923, says that the College 'has now veiled its identity under the title of Intercollegiate University', but it seems probable that it had done so long before that date.

[26]On Sibley and the Intercollegiate, see: Peter F Anson, *Bishops at Large*, Faber and Faber, London (1964), *passim*.

[27]Ibid., page 277. Anson also records that proceedings ended with a conjuring show.

Sulgrave', chartered in Delaware. This was so heavily ridiculed from the start, in both the press and by questions asked in Parliament, that it applied for the annulment of its charter almost at once, in 1945. The Sulgrave hoods are given in a correspondence between the Vice-chancellor and Registrar, the Revd Sidney Ernest Page Needham,[28] and Wippell's, and again, they could well be Franklyn's work.[29] Sulgrave was succeeded in its turn by the Western Orthodox Academy (later, University), chartered in 1945 by Hugh George Newman, acting in his capacity as 'Mar Georgius, Catholicos of the West';[30] this was also run by Needham. Its hoods are also likely to be Franklyn's work (see further page 52).[31]

More puzzling is the addition, on the title-page of the 1972 'Haycraft', of 'Hon: DLitt'. It is, perhaps, indicative that he lists it, not in large print after his name with his MA and MD, but in smaller type under his name, along with his fellowships. (Interestingly, the MA is not designated *hon: caus:*.) It does not appear on the title page of *Academical Dress*, and it is currently thought that it was awarded by the Central School of Religion, when he redesigned their robes.[32]

Fellowships of Learned Societies

Franklyn was also a Fellow of the Linnean Society (FLS): 'there are no pre-requisites for becoming a Fellow other than an active interest in natural history',[33] and a Fellow of the Society of Antiquaries of Scotland (FSA Scot),[34] for which one needs no more than 'an interest in the archaeology and history of Scotland', though both Societies require one to be proposed by existing Fellows. The point here is that, once he had completed his MB and Conjoint Diploma exams, in no case was any especial level of scholarly work required for any of his further 'sets of letters', including the MD(Lausanne) – although, of course, many Fellows of both the Linnean Society and the Society of Antiquaries of Scotland produce outstanding work in their fields. It is probable that he was hoping for an MA from Hull and from Southampton, but this did

---

[28] Church of England Rector of Farthinghoe 1925–46, but also Bishop of Mercia (Mar Theodorus) in the Old Catholic Orthodox Church. See further: ibid., page 374. *Crockford's*, of course, does not note his episcopacy. He seems to have occupied both posts without any problem, and died in 1962.

[29] I am grateful to Robin Richardson at Wippell for giving me a file of correspondence dealing with Sulgrave, from which this information is taken.

[30] 'His Beatitude Mar Georgius I, Patriarch of Glastonbury, Caertroia, and Mylapore; Successor of St Thomas, Apostolic-Pontiff of Celtica and of the Indies; Prince-Catholicos of the West, and of the United Orthodox Catholic Rite'. (Anson, *Bishops at Large*, page 444; other titles are listed on page 468.)

[31] The University seems to have ceased operations around 1977, until it was revived in 2015 by John Kersey, who had succeeded Newman. The Franklyn robes were replaced by a new scheme at that date.

[32] See pages 56–58.

[33] Linnean Society website.

[34] Franklyn invariably, and incorrectly, used the form 'FSA (Scot:)'. The Society is quite clear that the form to be used is FSA Scot (with the space before Scot), and lists the incorrect variants.

not happen.[35] He was also a Fellow of the Philosophical Society of England (FPhS), and may have had a hand in designing one of the several hoods used for that award.[36]

An interesting sidelight is provided by some letters between Franklyn and Francis Steer,[37] preserved in Steer's copy of *Academical Dress*.[38] Franklyn had gone to some lengths to acquire a copy for Steer, and sent him the duplicated letter which all recipients had. He added various manuscript comments, of which this sentence is germane:

> PS. Is it not odd that after producing the 4 books, 1964, 1968, 1969, and this in 1970 that no-one has bothered to elect me FRHistS or FSA?[39]

The wording is, perhaps, typical: 'no-one has bothered'. One imagines Franklyn sitting at home, waiting for the Hon: Sec: of one or other Society to write and say he had been elected a Fellow on account of his great eminence. But of course all his books, including *Academical Dress*, (but with the exception of *The Bearing of Coat-Armour by Ladies*, which was published by John Murray) were privately printed and published in exceedingly small runs, and he attempted to control very tightly exactly who might acquire copies, so his name was hardly going to be familiar to professional historians and antiquaries. Or was he fishing for Steer, who was both an FSA and an FRHistS, to nominate him?

Steer replied as follows.

> As to your recognition by the Royal Historical Society and/or the Society of Antiquaries, I'm surprised to learn you are not already a Fellow and I'm rather at a loss how best to advise you because fellowship of either body is strictly by personal

---

[35] Hull paid him 50 guineas instead – about £3000 in 2014.

[36] The Society had a very rocky patch, and was held in some disregard, but has ceased to award diplomas, and now describes itself as 'a group of enthusiasts who believe in the importance of exploring philosophical ideas and their relevance to our social and personal lives'. For the hood, see below, page 81.

[37] Francis William Steer, (1912–78), FSA, FRHistS. County Archivist for West Sussex, 1953–69; Archivist and Librarian of Arundel Castle, 1950–78; Archivist and Librarian of Chichester Cathedral, 1953–69; Archivist of New College, Oxford. He was also Archivist of the College of Arms, and was also appointed Maltravers Herald-Extraordinary by the Duke of Norfolk. He was awarded a Lambeth MA in 1959, in recognition of his work at Chichester; an Oxford MA in 1974 for his work at New College; and a DLitt by Sussex in 1978. See further ODNB (http://www.oxforddnb.com/view/article/57812.).

[38] The book is now in the possession of Dr Paul Coxon, to whom I am grateful for providing copies.

[39] The books were: *A genealogical history of the families of Paulet (or Pawlett), Berewe (or Barrow), Lawrence, and Parker* (Foundry Press, Bedford, December 1963) (printed privately, limited to 102 numbered and signed copies) and *Supplement to A genealogical history of the families of Paulet (or Pawlett), Berewe (or Barrow), Lawrence, and Parker* (W. E. Baxter, Lewes, Sussex, December 1968) (printed privately, limited to 150 numbered and signed copies). This takes care of the 1964 and 1968 ones; quite what the 1969 one was is unclear. (See List of Publications, page 117.)

recommendation and not by reputation alone. In other words, someone who has known you personally for a good many years must act as your prime nominator, and I'm sure that you could mention, with all the tact at your command, to such a friend (and you must have many) who is a Fellow of one or both of the Societies how much you would value election. This point is very difficult to express without appearing to be conceited, but the old rules are still strictly observed. If you can get a personal friend to nominate you, there would be no harm in giving him the names of other Fellows who you know personally or by reputation and would be willing to give their support. As I say, it is the personal approach which is essential and I don't think you should have any difficulty if one of your close friends will take the initiative.

It is hard to know quite how to read this. Did Steer genuinely assume that Franklyn had friends who were FRHistS and/or FSA? Or was Steer letting him down lightly, knowing he stood no chance? Whatever the case, Franklyn was never elected a Fellow of either body. Steer could presumably have proposed Franklyn for one or both of the Fellowships, but quite clearly did not wish to do so, hence the stress on '*close* friends'. This fits with the assessment given of Steer in his ODNB article: 'His manner was mild and courteously punctilious ...'

Did he hope for further recognition from London for his years of work in connexion with Convocation – possibly an MA? If so, he was disappointed, as nothing came his way.

4 The University of London

The University of London was a fixed centre of Franklyn's life. He was a member of the Standing Committee of Convocation from 1927 to 1942, and from 1932 to 1961 he was Bedell of Convocation.[1]

Until its abolition in 2003, Convocation had to approve changes in the academic dress of the University, and in many cases, it initiated such changes. The hand of Franklyn is known to be behind the choice of lilac for Veterinary Medicine, which he suggested as being 'the violet of Medicine diluted';[2] and also in the final form of the MTh robes, when that degree was introduced (see below).[3] He also designed the robes for the Bedells of Convocation – which (of course) 'look magnificent when in use'.[4]

As a Bedell himself he was noted for pulling incorrectly robed graduands out of the queue – an MB wearing an LL.B gown or vice versa was a noted bugbear with him, though to the graduand, then as now, it probably meant nothing.[5] All the odder, then, that in his summary of the robes on page 200 of *Academical Dress*, he says Medicine, Laws, and Music all wear the same gown, the sole difference being the slit behind for Laws: he does not note that the Medicine and Music gowns have the ends of the sleeves scalloped as on the MA gown (see Figure 3).[6] It is thus certain that he was behind the Report from a meeting of Convocation on 20 June 1920, in which Senate was:

> asked to call the attention of the University robemakers to the fact that at the last Degree Ceremony on Nov 24th, one or more medical graduates were seen to be wearing the gown prescribed for graduates in Laws, i.e., with a slit at the back,

[1] The Burgon Society Archive holds a collection of correspondence by Franklyn on London's academic dress, U/LOND/1/1; handlist available online: https://www.burgon.org.uk/wp-content/uploads/Burgon-Society-CAHF-papers-relating-to-the-Academical-Dress-of-the-University-of-London.pdf
[2] Franklyn, *Academical Dress*, page 199, note.
[3] Ibid., page 204.
[4] Ibid., page 205.
[5] The gowns are almost identical, being of the 'lay' [d4] pattern. The MB (and BMus) use it with the MA sleeve boot, while the LL.B wears it with a square boot and a slit behind. Small differences, likely to pass unnoticed in a crowded Albert Hall, which is where the presentation ceremonies were held.
[6] This lack of rigour appears all through his work.

Figure 3: London laws gown (left) and music and medicine gown (right)

and to provide some appropriate official of the University to see that the correct gown is worn on future occasions by medical graduates.[7]

These Minutes reveal the hand of Franklyn working through Convocation's recommendations to Senate. Section 2 of the same Minute reads:

> That in the opinion of this House, in the Regulations governing 'official and Academic Costume', it should be clearly laid down what caps or hats are to be worn for the various degrees, with undress or full dress costume, namely:[8]

and goes on to describe what they are to be. This is clearly Franklyn speaking, as the omission of prescribed hats annoyed him. This question was shelved owing to the war, but was revived in 1946, when 'Convocation requested that the Senate be asked to give effect to the recommendations forwarded by Convocation in June 1939 with regard to Academic Costume'.[9] The Senate Committee had in fact produced a revised form of the dress regulations, which included clarification on who might wear silk and who stuff gowns, and adding the option of the Oxford soft cap for women.

---

[7]Senate Minute 4396, July 1939, section 1. I am grateful to the Revd Philip Goff for providing extracts of the Senate Minutes that deal with questions of academic dress from 1837 onwards. Tracing Franklyn's influence during the relevant periods is comparatively easy from the wording.

[8]Senate Minute 4396, July 1939, section 2.

[9]Senate Minutes 3537–38, July 1946, section 1.

In 1940 Senate recommended the adoption of the MTh dress, which, as noted above, was Franklyn's work:

a) Hood, of black corded ottoman silk fully lined with the sarum red silk of the faculty, *the bottom of the cape portion being rounded.*

b) Gown, of black silk of the MA shape, with black cord, and sarum red covered button on the yoke (*all ecclesiastical degree gowns must be fitted with a cord and button on the yoke in order to keep the scarf in place*).

c) Cap, of the ordinary square black mortar-board type, with black tassel.[10]

Here, as so often, and as noted by the Registrar of Southampton, he cannot resist the temptation to lecture on what he considers to be correct usage.

In 1947, Senate was considering a proposal that the DDs should be permitted to wear 'a soft black square cap of black velvet (without tassel)'. This is explained as being 'the 'Pileus Quadratus' or doctoral cap of dignity which all Doctors in Theology have been entitled to wear'.[11] It was also suggested that the MTh should be permitted to wear that hat as well.[12] However, the Senate Committee over-ruled this, much to Franklyn's disgust: he was offended that the London DD wore (and still does) a black velvet Tudor bonnet – what he regarded as the hat of a lay doctor.

One thing dear to his heart, but which he also did not succeed in doing, was getting the MB hood 'upgraded'.[13] He was greatly upset that it was given a hood similar to all other bachelors – black, bordered inside the cowl with three inches of violet, the faculty colour, and the rest lined white – when it requires twice as long to qualify for.[14] Casting envious eyes at the Durham MB hood (scarlet, lined palatinate purple, the cape bound fur: 'the most beautiful bachelor hood in the world'), he wished the London MB to have a crimson hood bordered with three inches violet and lined white (see Figure 4).[15] He attempted to have the BDS visibly allied with Medicine when it was introduced in 1927 by giving it the MB,BS hood, with a three-inch border of violet, and having a new hood for the MB,BS, with a six-inch border of violet,[16] but this was rejected, and for reasons as yet unexplained, the BDS was given a three-inch border of olive green, which, as he rightly says, bears 'no relationship to anything whatsoever'.[17] (The other option, to give it a

---

[10] Senate Minutes 1021–22, June 1940. My emphases: they are the key to knowing it is Franklyn's work.

[11] Senate Minutes 4650–51, July 1947, section 2b.

[12] Senate Minutes 4650–51, July 1947, section 2e.

[13] It is a moot point whether this is the MB hood, or that for the MB and for the BS: as the degrees are never awarded separately, it is arguable that the BS(Lond) either has no hood, or uses the MB one.

[14] The white lining was restricted to members of Convocation until its abolition in 2003, since when all graduates have it.

[15] Franklyn, *Academical Dress*, page 204.

[16] Senate Minute 3109, May 1927, sections 1 and 2. But he never quite accepted that dentists stand on a par with other types of surgeon.

[17] Franklyn, *Academical Dress*, page 199. The BDS was the first London hood to use a shade of

different shade of violet, was eventually adopted in the case of the BVetMed in 1949, which uses lilac as its degree colour.) The BPharm (introduced in 1927), which he considered ought to have the BSc hood with an additional edging of medicine violet, was given old-gold, which does at least relate to the pale gold of Science. Both these hoods thus stay within the template for London bachelor hoods.

Figure 4: Franklyn's proposed MB hood

He was also concerned to get the Music hoods redone, as the pale blue BMus hood offended him, being, in his eyes, a Law hood. 'There is one freak hood in this University ... This blue hood for BMus is quite absurd, illogical, and bears no relation to anything'.[18] 'No-one knows why it was introduced!' – but he does not seem to have made the effort of going back through Senate and Convocation minutes to find out why.[19]

The degree was instituted in 1877, but robes were provided much earlier – possibly as the University wanted to award the DMus *honoris causa*.[20] The Minutes of the Committee on Academic Dress for 5 March 1861 simply record a suggestion for the Music degrees, with the BMus to have a hood of 'blue, lined with gold-coloured silk, with a single stripe of gold-coloured velvet: the degree is not mentioned before that date.[21] This hood was an exception, as the other bachelors wore hoods of black (BA), blue (LL.B), or violet (MB), with a three-inch border of velvet of the same colour, though at the same

---

green; it later appeared, as eau-de-nil, in Education hoods.

[18] Franklyn, *Academical Dress*, page 199.

[19] It would indeed be interesting to know why – and why various other late nineteenth-century/early twentieth-century universities have blue BMus hoods, while using black for all other bachelors: Wales, Belfast, Victoria, Liverpool – but not Birmingham, whose hoods otherwise conform to the London pattern.

[20] B Trowell, *Music*, in: *The University of London and the World of Learning 1836–1936*, ed. by F M L Thompson, Bloomsbury (1990) 183–208, page 193. This certainly happened at Wales, where the examined BMus was not awarded until 1905, but the DMus had been awarded *hon: caus:* since 1893.

[21] I am grateful to Prof Bruce Christianson for providing copies of the Minutes. Fifth Meeting, 5 March 1861, para 51 and 52.

meeting at which the BMus hood was suggested, it was also suggested that the others wear black hoods lined white with a border of velvet of faculty colour (which would have been mauve for BA, and scarlet for the newly-invented BSc) – so why should the BMus be lined gold? The BMus was also to have a blue gown of the same pattern as the BA one – again, with no reason for the colour change stated. The DMus was to wear scarlet lined with gold, a suggestion that it wear 'white brocaded silk' lined with gold being lost by 3 votes to 2.[22]

However, this BMus hood, which conformed to the original 1844 London scheme, then sank at the next meeting, as it was resolved that it was 'not, at present, expedient to make any provision for the Costume of Graduates in Music'. The current scheme of dress was voted in at the seventh meeting, on 8 April 1861, with no provision for music degrees.

The question was again considered at the eighth meeting (12 April 1861), when the DMus was given a blue silk gown of the flap-collar pattern [d4], and a blue silk hood lined with white watered silk. If a member of Convocation, then they could wear a scarlet gown and hood lined with white watered silk. The BMus was given identical robes to the non-Convocation DMus – blue silk [d4] gown and a blue silk hood, lined with white watered silk, with, it seems, no distinction being made for members of Convocation.[23] The blue was a dark blue, and not the light blue now used for the BMus. Indeed, the current MMus hood is the old BMus/DMus hood.[24] So yes, in one sense, 'no-one knows why it was introduced', as the Minutes are completely silent on the thinking behind both the blue gown and hood, and the white watered silk lining, and simply record the decision to approve them. However, the now familiar light blue hood was not introduced until 1910, when a minute for a meeting of Senate records:

> That the colour of the blue silk prescribed for the Robes of Graduates in Music be a light blue, instead of the very dark blue at present in use.[25]

The robes were then settled as:

DMus a scarlet gown with facings and sleeve-linings of white watered silk; a scarlet hood lined with white watered silk; an undress black gown of the same pattern as the MD.

BMus a light blue silk or black stuff gown of the MD pattern; a light blue silk hood bordered with three inches of white watered silk, or if a member of Convocation, fully lined with white watered silk.

---

[22]This exceptionally attractive set of robes did finally come to existence in George Shaw's scheme for Bath, although it is quite certain he did not know of this proposal.

[23]12 April 1861, para 99

[24]The MMus seems to have been introduced in the late 1960s – it is not in Shaw's book of 1966, but is in Smith's book of 1970. Trowell (op. cit.) does not mention it.

[25]Senate Meeting 16 March 1910, Minute no 1984, this being a report from the Standing Committee of Convocation.

Figure 5: London BMus (Convocation) gown and hood

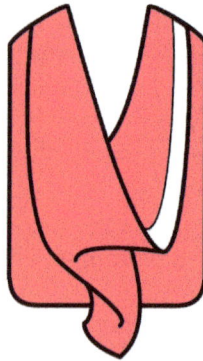

Figure 6: Franklyn's proposed BMus hood

Franklyn suggested that the BMus wear a cherry silk hood, bordered with three inches of white watered silk or brocade (see Figure 6), and that the DMus wear cream brocade lined with cherry, as the DMus scarlet robes also offended his sense of propriety.[26] The DMus was initially a 'freak', too: as we have seen, it wore a dark or mid-blue hood lined with white, with a blue gown

---

[26] He appears not to know of the 1861 suggestion (see above) for cream damask and gold. His suggestion, of course, would have created an equal 'freak', as he would have parachuted the Oxford DMus robes into the London scheme, which, as he so often said, is 'completely logical and symmetrical' – indeed, he implies it was the only one (presumably including his own schemes from Southampton and Hull) to exhibit these qualities. His suggested MB hood

– or scarlet and white robes if a member of Convocation. The logical BMus hood, black bordered with three inches white watered silk – or a new colour (for, as he rightly said, white was the Convocation colour), seems not to have occurred to him. As we have seen, the historically correct Convocation BMus hood was lined fully in white watered silk, and not with plain white bordered with watered white, as they are now usually made.[27]

So although Franklyn was heavily involved in the academic dress of London, not a single one of his proposed revisions came to pass, and his specification for the MTh was entirely predictable from the rest of the scheme.

---

would also have wrecked the symmetry.

[27]This is probably the result of robemakers applying the Convocation rule, and not seeing this exception, which was clearly noted. The Burgon Society Collection has a Convocation BMus blue gown and hood dating from c1960. The hood is fully lined white watered silk. See Figure 5.

5 Schemes of Academic Dress

Franklyn is well-known as the designer for four universities: Hull, Southampton, the Australian National University (ANU), and Malaya, as well as Chichester Theological College, and he had some input to the schemes at Nottingham, the New University of Ulster, and the Central School of Religion (CSR). He regularly boasted of his own academic dress designs as the most 'beautiful and dignified in the world'. This is best exemplified perhaps in the 'Prologue' of *Academical Dress*:

> ... the writer had the honour and privilege of designing a new hood for Chichester Theological College ... by far the most beautiful, dignified, and handsome theological hood in the world ... Southampton and Hull have the most beautiful, dignified, and perfect academical dress in Great Britain and Ireland, and Malaya (Singapore) the finest system of academical dress outside the British Isles.

In keeping with this, his favourite term for anything he disapproved of was 'freak'. It was somewhat unfortunate that he would promise a university the 'most beautiful and dignified robes in the world', only to make the same promise to another university a few years later.

Certain design features stand out, which enable a diagnosis of Franklyn's work to be made. One is the hood shape progression, from Burgon [s2] for bachelors, through London [f3] for masters, to Oxford full [f5] for doctors, and they are always fully lined. Each of these is usually used in his own 'improved' version of the shape: the 'improved London' has such a full cape that it is almost indistinguishable from the Oxford full. For Malaya, he states the cape is to be 'of full length (overall 45"; see Figures 7, 8 and 9 for comparison of the standard and 'improved' versions of the shapes).'[1] Another is the use of a 'university silk' to line all hoods – usually a light blue, though he originally suggested orange for Hull – and the faculty indicated by

---

[1] Frank W Haycraft, *The Degrees and Hoods of the World's Universities and Colleges*, ed. by Frederick R S Rogers et al., fifth edition, W E Baxter Ltd, Lewes, Sussex (1972), page 104. Wippell inform me that they had to take issue with him on this in regard to Southampton, as for graduates of short stature, a hood of this length would hang to their heels, if not drag on the ground, so a smaller size had to be approved. (Personal communication, Robin Richardson.) It was further helped by the fact that the Vice-Chancellor at the time was of short stature herself, and all that was needed was to put a Franklyn hood on her to make the point.

Figure 7: Standard [s2] hood, Oxford MA (left); Franklyn's 'improved' [s2] hood, Hull bachelor (right)

Figure 8: Standard [f3] hood, London MA (left); Franklyn's 'improved' [f3] hood, Hull master (right)

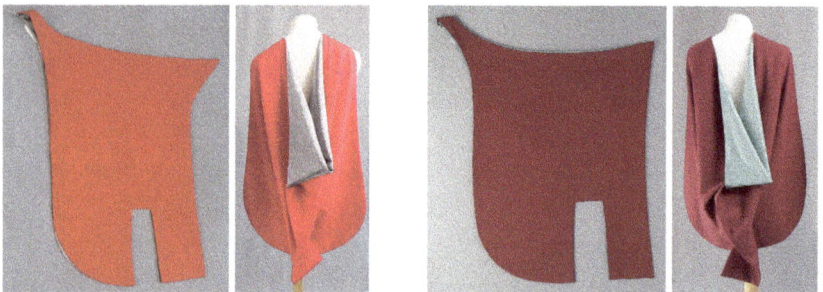

Figure 9: Standard [f5] hood, Oxford DLitt/DSc (left); Franklyn's 'improved' [f5] hood, Hull PhD (right)

coloured bindings. Gowns are usually London BA [b4] for bachelors; Oxford MA [m1] for masters; and Oxford [d2] for the doctors' dress robe. There are exceptions, of course: at Hull the faculty was indicated by coloured cords on the gowns, and the hoods left unbound; Ulster uses the Cambridge [f1] hood shape, which he hated, and is lined with dark green; Nottingham has part-lined bachelors' hoods; Malaya does not use a university lining; and there is the extreme oddity of making Hull's musicians (alone) wear the Oxford gimp gown. The scheme for the Central School of Religion (*vide infra*) reverses the pattern, and has the hoods lined with faculty colour and bound with the School colour (old gold). It was these features that enabled the identification of the following early schemes as his work.

Early and hitherto unknown schemes

Franklyn's earliest schemes, about which he subsequently remained silent, were for the degrees awarded by an *episcopus vagans*. This has only come to light by means of a certain amount of detective work.

In the back of the British Library's lending copy of the 1927 edition of 'Haycraft',[2] there are some MS notes on the hoods for 'degrees' awarded by various autonomous bishops and churches.[3] I posted these on the Yahoo! academic dress group,[4] and in doing so certain terminology in one of them caught my eye: specifically, the scheme for the 'English Episcopal Church (Independent), St John, Madras', with the date 1948 appended. This led me to consider Franklyn as the designer, and for various other reasons, to be examined below, this can now be accredited as his work.

The scheme reads as follows (see Figure 10 for sketches of the hoods):

> ***Bachelors' hoods (except BD)*** are made in the improved Burgon shape [s2], in black corded silk, lined faculty colour silk, edged 1" apple blossom silk.
>
> ***Masters' and BD hoods*** are made in an improved London shape [f3], in black corded silk, lined faculty colour silk, and bound on all edges 1" apple blossom silk.
>
> ***Doctors' hoods*** are made in the Oxford full shape [f5], in scarlet cloth lined faculty colour silk, and bound 1" apple blossom silk.
>
> ***Faculty colours***
> > ***Arts and Letters*** cardinal red.
> > ***Theology*** purple (but BD lined black);
> > ***Laws*** light blue;
> > ***Civil Law*** dark blue;
> > ***Music*** pink;
> > ***Philosophy*** light green.

I suggested that various factors 'ineluctably draw one to conclude that Dr Franklyn had a hand in this system'. These are four in number.

---

[2] Haycraft, *Degrees and Hoods (1927)*. This particular copy is available through the county library inter-library lending system.

[3] Similar annotations, in the same hand, are made in a copy of the 1924 edition, which belonged to Frederick Rogers and is now in the possession of Dr Alex Kerr, to whom I am grateful for supplying copies of the relevant pages. There are reasons for believing the hand is that of Haycraft himself.

[4] Message no 29899, 10 May 2010.

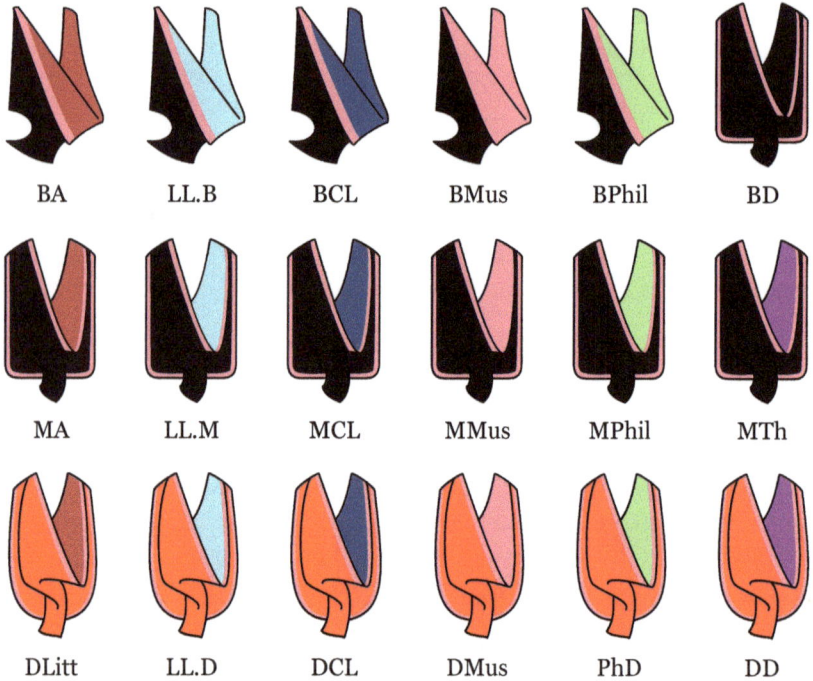

| BA | LL.B | BCL | BMus | BPhil | BD |

| MA | LL.M | MCL | MMus | MPhil | MTh |

| DLitt | LL.D | DCL | DMus | PhD | DD |

Figure 10: Hoods of the English Episcopal Church

First, the use of the terms 'improved Burgon' and 'improved London'. This is a trademark 'Franklynism', and it is to be found in at least three of the schemes which he is known to have designed, *vidz*, Hull,[5] Southampton,[6] and Malaya.[7] He disliked the standard version of these shapes, and designed his own 'improved' – i.e., more generously cut – patterns.

Second, the shape progression from bachelor to doctor, again to be found at Hull, Southampton, and Malaya. Bachelors have Burgon [s2] hoods, masters London [f3] ones, and doctors Oxford full [f5]. The use of a full shape for the BD is also diagnostic: he did the same at Hull.[8]

Third, the choice of faculty colours. Franklyn had drawn up a list of what he considered to be the 'correct English' faculty colours, which was:[9]

---

[5] Haycraft, *Degrees and Hoods (1972)*, page 10.

[6] Ibid., page 18.

[7] Ibid., page 104.

[8] Although there the BD is given, as at Oxford, the doctors' pattern [f5] rather than the masters' pattern.

[9] No single reference will suffice, as the evidence is scattered throughout Franklyn's writings. In compiling this list he was somewhat like Dr Dearmer and his 'English' liturgical colours, though Dearmer was arguing from a stronger position of fact.

Divinity black	***Music*** pink
Laws mid-blue	***Science*** grey
Medicine crimson	***Letters*** light blue
Arts none as such	***Philosophy*** green

Certainly Laws, Music, and Philosophy fit this. Purple for Theology does not fit quite so well. He gave it scarlet at Hull. Southampton uses violet, but it is not clear if this choice was his, or that of the university or the robemakers: the BTh and MTh were introduced after his death, but he may have made provision in the original scheme. On the other hand, his unadopted 'universal' theological college hood was black, lined dark violet silk, and bound scarlet cloth (see Figure 11).[10] For the University of Malaya he used light cerise for Arts (as at Southampton), blue for Laws, and light green for Philosophy. The use of 'apple blossom' instead of 'pink' also implies someone with a close knowledge of academic dress: the term is used solely at Liverpool for its Arts faculty colour. (See Appendix 1, page 82, for a comparative table of faculty colours.)

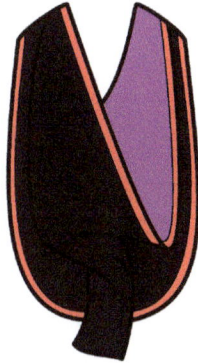

Figure 11: Franklyn's 'universal' theological college hood

The Divinity hoods are interesting in this context, as the faculty colour is not carried through from bachelor through master to doctor. The DD and MTh are lined with purple, which is stated as the faculty colour, but the BD with black, giving the BD a very understated hood of black lined black, with a 1" pink border. This is not something that one expects in a Franklyn scheme, as logical progression from one grade to the next was almost an obsession with him, and thus the BD should be lined purple. But, as it is the same shape as the MTh, the two hoods would be identical, though this would be avoided by giving the BD the [f5] shape, as at Oxford and as he later did at Hull.

Fourth is the design of the hoods: black (scarlet for doctors) lined with faculty colour, and bound with a 'university silk'. The use of a university

---

[10] Franklyn, *Academical Dress*, page 214. But there he states that the scarlet cloth is to show that 'the wearer is a theologian and in holy orders'. Quite how it does so is beyond the wit of the present writer, as scarlet cloth is normally associated with doctors.

silk was another Franklynism. At Southampton (peacock blue) and Ulster[11] (dark green) it lines the hoods, which are bound with faculty colour; at Hull (turquoise) it lines the hoods, but they are not bound with faculty colour. For the English Episcopal Church, of course, the 'university' silk (apple-blossom pink) forms the binding, and the faculty silk the lining.

Finally, there is the date. Franklyn designed the Southampton robes in 1952, and those for Hull in 1954. In 1948, Nottingham gained a charter, and it is generally accepted that Franklyn had some input into that system too.[12] But 1948 was also the date of his first-known design, the revised (and at the time controversial) hood for Chichester Theological College.[13]

As the notes are in a 'hood book', nothing is said about the gowns. But as has been demonstrated, Franklyn is nothing if not predictable (or, as he would say, logical). Both Southampton and Hull use the same gown progression, and it is therefore highly likely that it was used for the English Episcopal Church. This would put the bachelors in a black London BA gown [b4], quite possibly with faculty colour cords and buttons on the sleeves and yoke;[14] the masters in a black Oxford MA gown [m1], again with a faculty colour cord and button on the yoke; and the doctors in a scarlet Oxford dress robe [d2], with either faculty colour sleeves and facing, and an apple-blossom cord and button on the yoke; or apple-blossom sleeves and facings and a faculty colour cord and button on the yoke – I suggest the former is more likely.

Taken all in all, I thought it was entirely likely that this scheme might well be an early piece of work by Franklyn. But we can go further and definitely tie it to him, as he knew the founder of the English Episcopal Church, which was established about 1944 by the late Bishop Charles Leslie Saul.[15] Around 1980, it changed its name to the Protestant Evangelical Reformed Church.[16] Quite what the '(Independent)' signifies is not clear, but most likely it is a 'note to self' by the writer of the MS notes to remind him that it is independent of any other church. The words 'St John' may refer to the University of St John,[17] which, along with the Western Orthodox Academy (later University;

---

[11] Franklyn laid out the principles of this system, but it is not totally his work. Apart from anything else, it uses the square-cornered Cambridge [f1] shape, which he detested, and hoped to get 'rectified' to a round-caped hood. See Franklyn, *Academical Dress*, page 209ff and Haycraft, *Degrees and Hoods (1972)*, page 28.

[12] Principally getting the hood shape changed from [s1] to [f1]. It, too, uses a 'university silk' (light blue) with faculty colour bindings. See Franklyn, *Academical Dress*, page 208.

[13] The design is of interest: Oxford full [f5], black rayon, lined grey poplin, and bordered inside the cowl with 3 inches, and bound on the cape with 1 inch, rose nylon.

[14] This was the case at both Hull (until 1989) and Southampton (until 1993) - and also for their masters and doctors. He also specified a London BA gown for Chichester, with rose-colour cords and button on sleeves and yoke.

[15] On Saul and his churches, see further Anson, *Bishops at Large*, page 232ff.

[16] I am grateful to Prof William Hughes for this information. The denomination also used a number of very similar titles, such as Protestant Evangelical Church of England. Saul died in 1991, but a very small number of congregations still exists.

[17] Anson, *Bishops at Large* refers in passing (page 457) to this institution as being associated with the Western Orthodox Academy, and attracting hostility.

see below), attracted unwelcome attention, and both of which were chartered in India.

At much the same time that I was working on this material, Sqn-Ldr Alan Birt wrote to me, without knowing I was doing so, to say that he had just found an undated copy of the prospectus of the London College of Theology, at the time a well-known bogus college in existence from the late 1940s to the mid-1950s, whose hood was listed in *Hoodata* 1.1 (Spring 1974).[18] Because of its Hoodata entry, I knew of the existence of the College and its hood: what I had not known, but was revealed in the prospectus, is that the Warden of the College was Bishop Saul, and the 'Adviser on Academical Dress and Ceremonial' was Charles Franklyn. This makes a definite link between Saul and Franklyn, and thus the EEC hoods can be moved from 'probably Franklyn's work' to 'definitely Franklyn's work'. As noted above, it forms one of, if not the, earliest scheme by him on record, and is thus of great interest as exhibiting a number of features which were to appear in subsequent schemes by him. The only thing that is missing is a definite date, though we can posit 1944.

Under its name of the Protestant Evangelical Reformed Church, the church awarded diplomas in theology through its training institution, Cranmer Hall.[19] The hoods were London shape [f3], black lined grey, bordered inside the cowl with purple (ATh: one inch; LTh: two inches; FTh: three inches).[20] The similarity to both the Chichester hood and the London bachelor's hood will be noticed.

Two further schemes are listed in the MS notes. One is for 'Glastonbury Degrees', or 'degrees conferred by the Primate of the Western Orthodox Catholic Church, 1951' – i.e., Hugh George de Wilmott Newman (Mar Georgius, Patriarch of Glastonbury and Catholicos of the West).[21] Only doctorates were

---

[18] Not to be confused with the London College of Divinity (now St John's College, Nottingham) or the London School of Theology (*olim* the London Bible College). The hood was [s1], black, lined grass green silk – odd, as Franklyn hated the [s1] shape. The right to wear it was effectively given on payment of a fee. On the various colleges mentioned in this section, see Nicholas Groves, ed., *Shaw's Academical Dress of Great Britain and Ireland*, vol. 2: *Non-Degree-Awarding Bodies*, third edition, Burgon Society (2014), pages 144, 147, 149 and 150.

[19] Not the same as Cranmer Hall at Durham, which is part of St John's College. Saul's college is still functioning, though no longer attached to the PECE, as Cranmer Memorial Bible College and Seminary, and uses totally different academic dress, though black and grey figure quite largely in it. There was also a College Hood for non-graduates who had completed the General Ordination Examination of the Church: Cambridge full [f1], black, the cowl bordered 1" Cambridge blue. It was approved by the Convocation of the PECE in 1936.

[20] Thus two undated prospectuses in my possession, one with and one without the FTh. *Hoodata* vol 1, no 8, summer 1977, says the shape was Burgon.

[21] Hugh George de Wilmott Newman, 1905–1979. He was the General Manager and Secretary of the National Association of Cycle Traders and Repairers (Anson, *Bishops at Large*, page 451). He collected no fewer than twenty-three lines of episcopal succession, and is viciously parodied as the episcopus vagans Mr Skegg ('Mar Sylvestrius') in A N Wilson's 1978 novel *Unguarded Hours*. These 'degrees', although doubtless intended as a parallel to Lambeth degrees, were awarded on no authority other than his own.

awarded, and the hoods were full shape (exact pattern unspecified, but if, as I suspect, these also are Franklyn's work, then probably Oxford full), in purple, lined with gold silk, and bound with faculty colour (see Figure 12). Again, this use of the 'university lining' with faculty bindings might indicate Franklyn's hand. The faculty colours were:

> **DChr** black corded silk; [*Doctor Christianissimus*]
> **DD** black plain silk;
> **STD** black watered silk; [*Sacræ Theologiæ Doctor*]
> **DSS** mauve; [probably *Doctor in Scriptura Sacra*]
> **LL.D** pale blue;
> **DCL** dark blue;
> **DJur** turquoise; [Doctor of Jurisprudence]
> **MD** scarlet;
> **MusD** cherry;
> **PhD** sage green;
> **DPhil** apple green;[22]
> **DLitt** crimson;
> **DSc** silver grey;
> **DPed** white; [Doctor of Pedagogy]
> **DArch** russet. [Doctor of ?Architecture, ?Archæology]

The use of different shades of the same colour for related degrees will be noted. In the case of the Divinity degrees, the difference is marked by various types of finish of the lining.

Figure 12: Glastonbury DChr/DD/STD hood

Another list is for degrees of the 'Western Orthodox University, 1945' (the successor to the 'Intercollegiate University', for which he also designed a set of robes). Here again the hoods follow the Franklyn progression from Burgon via London to Oxford full (see Figure 13).[23]

---

[22] Quite what the difference between the PhD and DPhil was is unclear – if indeed there was one. Likewise between DCL, LL.D, and DJur, and DD and STD. Possibly the choice of the recipient.
[23] The 1924 MS notes have degrees in the faculties of Arts (BA, MA; peon [sic] red); Divinity

Bachelors Burgon shape [s2], black, lined dove grey, bordered 2" fur and 3" faculty silk.

Masters London shape [f3], black, lined faculty colour silk.

Doctors Oxford full shape [f5], scarlet lined faculty colour silk.

Faculty colours

Arts peony red;
Commerce pale blue;
Divinity crimson;
Laws dark blue;
  DCL light blue;
  DCanL powder blue;
  DJur navy blue;
International Law turquoise

Letters old gold;
Music lavender;
Pedagogy grey;
Philosophy green.
Science violet
'DSS' black.
  (Probably Doctor in Sacred Scripture, not in Social Science).

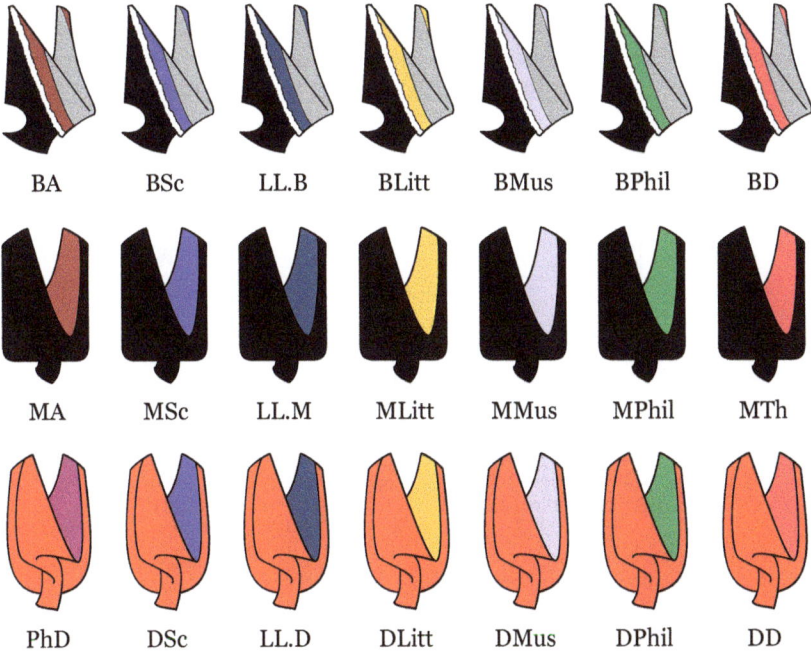

Figure 13: Hoods of the Western Orthodox University

On the one hand, one might have expected the dove grey lining of the bachelors' hoods to carry over as a 'university silk', but on the other, this parallels

(BD, MTh, DD; crimson); Letters (BLitt, MLitt, DLitt; old gold); Music (MusB, MusM, MusD; lavender); Laws (LL.B, LL.M, LL.D; dark blue); Science (MSc, DSc; violet); Philosophy (BPhil, MPhil, DPhil: green); Natural Philosophy (PhD; cerise).

the University of London use, where the bachelors have a black hood, part-lined faculty silk, and the rest lined white.[24] The fur is an anomaly, and may have been included at the request of the 'University' or of the Patriarch; Franklyn never used fur in any of his known schemes. Given that, as noted above, Mar Georgius and Bishop Saul knew each other, it could well be that Franklyn, having designed for one, was asked to do so for the other.

These are not the same body. Mar Georgius' Catholic Apostolic Church chartered the 'Western Orthodox Academy' in 1945 in succession to the former 'University of Sulgrave'. This 'University' had attracted much opprobrium, including questions in Parliament, and attacks in the Spectator, the Cambridge Review, and the News Review, insinuating that the degrees granted 'though possibly legal, were worthless'.[25] It was founded c.1940, and named from the village of Sulgrave in Northants, which was the home of the ancestors of George Washington. Chartered in Delaware, it applied for annulment of its charter around 1946.[26] It was itself a successor to the Intercollegiate University (see below; also Anson, Bishops at Large, pp 374–5.) Another fortuitous communication, this time from Wippell, contained a package of papers relating to Sulgrave, dated 1942, dealing with samples of silk for the faculty colours, though the samples were not included.[27] The letters reveal that Sulgrave used lavender for music, cerise for philosophy, old gold for letters, and violet for science: these are almost the same as the Western Orthodox colours, save for Philosophy, which has changed from Sulgrave's crimson to the WOU's green. Doctors' hoods were of scarlet cloth lined edge to edge with faculty colour, and masters' black lined edged to edge with faculty colour, but the full scheme (shapes, etc) is lacking. A hood for the DLitt was made for a Francis J Griffiths of Irthlingborough, and a PhD hood for 'the Revd Sherley-Price'.[28]

---

[24] Franklyn was, of course, a graduate of London, and a vociferous member of its Convocation, especially where academic dress was concerned. See also the 1948 Chichester Theological College hood, and the diploma hoods of the Protestant Evangelical Reformed Church noted above, which also have grey linings and coloured borders. He also suggested, reasonably enough, that the bachelors' hoods of Birmingham and Exeter should follow London use, and be lined with white in addition to their faculty borders.

[25] Anson, Bishops at Large, page 457. It is worth recalling that until the Education Reform Act of 1992, it was legal for any body (or, indeed, anybody) to grant degrees, though those not awarded by recognized universities (of which there were in any case far fewer, thus making identification of the bogus ones easier) were usually pilloried in the press. The sole reason that London University (founded 1828, now UCL) did not award degrees was, not that it did not have a royal charter, but, as Mr Bickersteth informed Lord Brougham when the latter asked what was to prevent it awarding degrees without a charter, 'The universal scorn and contempt of mankind'. (Report of the Privy Council Board on London University's application for a royal charter, May 11, 1834, in the Greville Memoirs.)

[26] Ibid., page 457.

[27] The fact that Wippell was involved might point to Franklyn: as we shall see, he regarded them as the best robemakers 'in the world'. See below for his annoyance over Ede & Ravenscroft getting the Hull account and not Wippell – owing, it has to be said, to his own over-insistence.

[28] There are two of this name in the 1956 Crockford's. I am assuming it is Lionel Digby Sherley-Price, because the correspondence with Wippell says he needs his hood as soon as possible, 'as he may be ordered to the high seas at any moment'. (Letter, SET Needham to Wippell, 1

The Intercollegiate University (College of Church Musicians), domiciled in Kansas, which preceded the University of Sulgrave, was a notorious degree-mill,[29] founded in 1890, and was closed by about 1940. It had a highly idiosyncratic scheme (see Appendix 2, page 83), but the 1927 MS notes (probably in Franklyn's hand) have a revision 'from 1st June 1938'. All hoods were full, 'with rounded cape' (note that).

Bachelors black, bound 2" fur on all edges, and 2.5" faculty silk inside.

Masters black, lined and bound 0.25" faculty silk.

Doctors scarlet, lined and bound 0.75" faculty silk.

Faculty colours

Arts damask red;[30]	**Music** gold;
Divinity crimson;	**Philosophy** bronze green.
Civil Law royal blue;	**Letters** white
Laws pale blue;	**Commerce** emerald
Medicine fuchsia red;	green.[31]

This is quite certainly Franklyn's work. As we have seen from his entries in The Medical Directory from 1940 onwards, he was awarded an MA honoris causa by the Intercollegiate University, which we may take as reward for doing this – exactly as he was awarded an MA by Malaya later.

The Western Orthodox Academy was incorporated as the 'Western Orthodox University' in India under Act XXI of 1860 on 20 February 1950, although, as noted above, it had been active since 1945. (The degrees known, from the title assumed by de Wilmott Newman, as 'Glastonbury degrees' were a separate set of awards).[32] Anson remarks tartly that:

A Doctorate of Divinity could be obtained for £15 15s; a Master-ship of Arts for £10 10s. Full particulars of the most attractive Faculty Gowns, Hoods, Caps and bands could be obtained from the Registrar.[33]

October 1942.) Sherley-Price was an MA of Sidney Sussex College, Cambridge (1936), and trained at Chichester. After a curacy at Ryde, he served as a naval chaplain, and in 1942 was indeed summoned to the high seas, aboard HMS *Unicorn*. He served the rest of his ministry within the Navy. I have not been able to trace Dr Griffiths.

[29] So much so that a Norwich clergyman, Robert Middleton, Vicar of St Martin-at-Oak and Rector of St Miles Coslany from 1891 to 1919, who acquired the degrees of BD and DLitt from the College, had them listed in *Crockford's* that year, but they were removed in all following editions. He was then Vicar of St Matthew, Rugby, from 1919 to 1931. Articles in the local press poke fun at his degrees, which suggests that he continued to use them.

[30] *sic*: it is not clear if this means red damask/brocade, or a specific shade of red.

[31] A list of faculty colours for the Intercollegiate on the back of a letter from Needham to Wippell, 16 October 1942, adds violet for Science; and gives the Divinity colour as 'crimson shot', Laws as 'azure', and Civil Law as 'dark blue'.

[32] See further http://www.liberalcatholics.org/education.html. The notes in Dr Kerr's copy state 'Western Orthodox University (founded 1945) (Ambur, India)'.

[33] Anson, *Bishops at Large*, page 457, and see above, pages 52–54. The Registrar, who was also the Chancellor, was 'Mar Theodorus, Bishop of Mercia' – otherwise known as Sidney

A further listing in the MS notes in the 1924 edition is for the 'Western International University, USA'. This appears to have been founded in 1952, and is noted as 'discontinued 1959'. The similarity of the hoods to those of both the WOU and London University (again reading white for grey in the bachelors' hoods) will be noted:

> **Bachelors** full shape, black, lined grey, bordered 4" faculty colour.
> **Masters** full shape, black lined faculty colour.
> **Doctors** full shape, scarlet lined faculty colour.
> **Faculty colours**
>
> | | |
> |---|---|
> | **Arts** crimson; | **Music** lavender; |
> | **Divinity** scarlet; | **Letters** old gold; |
> | **Laws** dark blue; | **Philosophy** green. |

Was this yet another reincarnation of the Western Orthodox Academy/ University?

So, having established a definite connexion between Saul and Franklyn via the London College of Theology, there can be no doubt but that the other schemes are his work also. It is instructive that he makes absolutely no reference to these schemes later in his life.

There remains the curiosity of Franklyn's DLitt. It does not appear on the title page of the 1970 Academical Dress, but it does on that of the 1972 Degrees and Hoods, where he lists himself as

> Charles A. H. Franklyn, M.A., M.D.,
> Hon: D.Litt., F.L.S., F.S.A. (Scot:)

It is worth noting the layout, with the DLitt included in smaller type along with his fellowships, which may suggest that he did not wish to draw too much attention to it, possibly implying that he felt its source was not entirely reputable. It is also clearly marked as an honorary award (unlike the MA, which too was awarded honoris causa – by Malaya, when he designed their robes – or was he hiding it behind the 'full' MA from Lincoln-Jefferson University?). It is unclear where he gained it, though a tradition persists that it was awarded by the Central School of Religion,[34] and if so, may be another 'reward' for designing their new set of robes; equally it may well be the reward for the 'Glastonbury' robes.

EP Needham, Rector of Farthinghoe, a village a few miles from Sulgrave; Anson, *Bishops at Large*, page 374. Needham retained his Anglican cure while carrying out episcopal functions as an *episcopus vagans*. Unfortunately, Anson does not give a reference for the source of this information. Needham was also Acting Registrar and later Pro-Vice-Chancellor of the University of Sulgrave. The Western Orthodox University was revived in 2015 by John Kersey, who had succeeded to the titles of 'Primate of the Apostolic Episcopal Church' and 'Catholicos of the West'. A new set of robes was designed in that year by Kersey, thus consigning the Franklyn designs to history. But one suspects that very few of the robes were made in any case.

[34] Personal communication, the Revd Dr Mark Gretason. The documentation which would clarify this is currently inaccessible.

The Central School of Religion (CSR) is the successor of a correspondence institute called Central University, which was incorporated in Indiana in 1896.[35] As a result of success of its School of Religion at the expense of the other parts of the University, and also in order to maintain the independence of the School from state control of its programmes, Central University changed its name to Central School of Religion in 1947. In 1967, charge of CSR passed to Dr Douglas Geary, who lived in the UK, and control remains in the UK. CSR absorbed the Faculty of Church Music in 1968.

Haycraft 1927 gives its hoods as following the American Intercollegiate Code, with a lining of 'blue with scarlet strip in the centre' and a white chevron.[36] In the 1972 edition it is not listed under Indiana:[37] it appears in the UK section, under 'Colleges of Theology (Other Denominations)'.[38] The hoods listed there are:

ATh Black stuff bound with 1" old gold silk. Simple.

LTh Black stuff lined with black silk, and bound with 2" old gold silk. Simple.

ThSoc Black silk fully lined with old gold silk. Simple.[39]

Honorary Doctorates In the Leeds DD pattern,[40] and of scarlet cloth lined with satin of the Faculty colour, and with 1" binding of old gold silk. The entire hood is edged with 1" of old gold silk.

Faculty Colours

DD Crimson		**DLitt** Green	
DCanL Purple		**DHum** White.	
LL.D Dark blue			

Alternatively, the American Intercollegiate Code may be followed, with hoods lined and edged with old gold.

The doctoral dress robes are of the Cambridge MusD pattern [d3], in scarlet, with facings and cuffs to match the hood lining, but they do not have any gold on them.[41]

It is known that these robes were introduced around 1970. They were later added to with hoods for bachelors (simple [s1]) and masters (full, [f1]), both of black lined faculty colour and bound gold. It is at present unclear when

---

[35]There is, or was, another Central University, in Kentucky.

[36]Haycraft, *Degrees and Hoods (1927)*, page 50, *s.v.* Central University. All other editions omit 'in the centre'. This meant that the lining is blue, with a white chevron, and a narrow scarlet border along the cowl edge in addition to the faculty velvet.

[37]Although a Central Scientific College is.

[38]Haycraft, *Degrees and Hoods (1972)*, page 38. The entire section is initialled CAHF.

[39]The ATh and LTh have always been made in the Oxford simple shape [s1], while the ThSoc (Theologiæ Socius - Fellow in Theology) has always been Burgon shape [s2].

[40]This is a variant of the Cambridge shape [f1], in which the cowl does not hang to the base of the cape when worn.

[41]For the full specification, see Groves, *Shaw's Academical Dress II: Non-Degree-Awarding Bodies*, page 139.

the lower degrees were introduced, but even if their hoods are not directly designed by Franklyn, it would have been easy enough to extrapolate them from the doctoral hoods.

Chichester Theological College

This hood provides yet another example of Franklyn ignoring what he wished not to see. Chichester's first hood[42] – full shape, black, lined violet, and bound fur – fell foul of the 1882 Act of Convocation, which restricted theological colleges to black stuff hoods of Oxford simple or Cambridge shape, with a border of up to 2" of a coloured silk. Chichester's was changed to black, Cambridge shape, bound on all edges with 1" Oxford MA shot crimson, which was later changed to a red cord.[43] The reason for the 1948 change was because 'there was much discontentment with the poor little thing, the existing hood'.[44] Franklyn's description of how it was introduced to the College deserves quoting:

> Having designed the hood and had it made, the writer went over to Chichester with many robes and borrowing some twenty students of the College a demonstration of robes was given … the procession going round the large room in front of the Principal and members of the Council. When the wearer of the new hood reached the Principal he said 'Stop: is that it'?[45]

From the Principal's reaction, it seems that there was no consultation over the design, and it is unclear why those particular colours were chosen. According to Franklyn's account, it was thought by the Principal and others to be 'splendid', and it was taken across to the bishop, who approved it 'at once'. It is, of course, 'the most handsome, dignified, and beautiful theological college hood in the world and is the pride of her *alumni*'. The college closed in 1994, so it will gradually be less and less seen.

Franklyn's design was Oxford full shape [f5], in black ribbed rayon, lined with grey poplin, and bordered inside the cowl with 3 inches, and bound on the cape with 1 inch, of rose nylon (see Figure 14). It was criticized for breaking the terms of the 1882 Act, as it had a full lining. Franklyn responded by referring to Canon 58 of 1603, which requires literates to wear black 'tippets', so long as they are not of silk. He maintained (quite accurately) that his hood was not made of silk, but used man-made fibres: 'This most handsome hood does not infringe the Archbishop of Canterbury's wishes in regard to Theological College hoods, no silk being employed at all'. But he was of

---

[42] The date of introduction is unclear. It is not in Wood's book of 1875, but is in his 1882/3 one, as is the revised hood.

[43] The exact date and the reason for the change to cord have yet to be established: it had happened by 1923.

[44] Franklyn, *Academical Dress*, page 214.

[45] Ibid. He gives the Principal as JRH Moorman, who later became Bishop of Ripon.

Figure 14: Franklyn's hood for the Chichester Theological College

course ignoring the provision which the 1882 Act imposed, *vidz*, that the hood might have only a narrow (up to two inches) border of silk, and not be fully lined.[46]

'The most beautiful and dignified hoods ...'

Between 1948 and 1956 Franklyn designed complete systems of academic dress for the universities of Malaya in Singapore (for which he was awarded an MA honoris causa in 1951), Southampton, Hull, and the Australian National University, as well as Chichester Theological College. At various times he contributed to the academic dress schemes of several other universities (in particular, the universities of Cambridge and of Nottingham, and the New University of Ulster). He was quite certainly the designer, if not the prime mover, in the MD robes for Lausanne. It is unlikely that he had anything to do with those of Bruxelles, owing to the dates. So far as Bruxelles is concerned, he remarks on page 211 of *Academical Dress* that when it was granting the MD,[47] between 1880 and 1920, that 'Robes were then established for their use'. These were a dress robe of Cambridge pattern [d1], in scarlet cloth,

---

[46]The only other fully-lined theological college hoods in use at this time were those of Queen's College, Birmingham, which hood was never officially sanctioned by the College anyway, but was designed by the students; and Coates Hall, Edinburgh, which served the Episcopal Church in Scotland, and thus did not come within the remit of the 1882 Act. A number of other fully-lined hoods appeared after the 1948 Chichester one – Wells, Salisbury, Trinity College Bristol, etc. It has be said that some of the bordered hoods were made with a black lining, thus possibly breaking the Act.

[47]See also page 28 *supra*.

faced and the sleeves lined light blue silk; a hood of Cambridge shape 'but the cape rounded at the bottom' – so more like a Durham full shape [f7], in scarlet cloth, lined light blue silk; and a black velvet bonnet with light blue cords and tassels. Quite how official these robes ever were is a moot point.

Doctors of Medicine of the University of Lausanne

Figure 15: Franklyn wearing the Lausanne MD robes

These robes can, I think, be accounted a Franklyn design, although he is very coy about it in *Academical Dress*. 'Steps were taken to secure a distinctive silk'; Ede & Ravenscroft 'were approached'; the silk was found, sent to the university and sealed. The silk was a 'virgin blue' watered silk. Although he acknowledges 'the late Dr Frédéric Wanner, Privat Docent de l'Université' for getting the silk sealed, I think that the passive voice of the approach conceals Franklyn. This was more ambitious scheme than that for the Bruxelles MDs, who had a robe and hood. Besides a hood of scarlet cloth lined with the blue silk, (Oxford as to cape, Cambridge as to cowl, so Durham again), there was a dress robe of Oxford style, faced and sleeves covered with the blue silk; a convocation habit to match;[48] and an undress gown (Oxford MA, with two rows of gimp round each armhole.) There were two hats: a black square for use with the undress gown and convocation habit, and a black velvet bonnet with blue cords and tassels for use in full dress. These robes, with the change

---

[48]The Burgon Society possesses Franklyn's own habit, via the late Dr George Shaw.

to turquoise silk, (and the omission of the convocation habit) were to be reproduced almost exactly for the higher doctors at Hull in the 1950s. As will be seen below, the use of light blue silk linings, and the obsession with an 'improved' Oxford hood shape are 'Franklynisms'. See Figure 15 for pictures of Franklyn wearing these robes.

He lists also, in *Academical Dress*, robes for four doctorates at Göttingen: hood and robe shapes exactly as Oxford, but the DD lined and faced with black silk, the LL.D with purple, the MD with crimson, and the PhD with violet, although how official these hoods were is not known: possibly, like the Lausanne robes, they were invented for graduates who needed a hood. Whether Franklyn had anything to do with this is not known, but it would seem at least possible.

The University of Malaya

Figure 16: Franklyn wearing the Malaya MA hood

The University was established by the British Government in October 1949, and had two divisions: the University of Malaya in Singapore, now the National University of Singapore, and the University of Malaya in Kuala Lumpur, now simply the University of Malaya.[49] Franklyn designed the 'complete

---

[49] Both universities have retained these robes, but have adapted them as new degrees have been added. See: Smith, *Academical Dress and Insignia*, page 447 for Malaya and page 499 for Singapore. The current Singapore forms can be seen at https://nus.edu.sg/commence-

system of Academical and Official Dress' in May 1949.[50] It is not known how he came by the commission.

Figure 17: Hoods of the University of Malaya

The scheme is simple, and follows what we have seen is his standard shape-progression, with bachelors having 'improved' Burgon hoods, masters London ones ('45 inches long'), and doctors Oxford full. Bachelors and masters have a 'dark blue' hood, fully lined with faculty colour, though the picture of Franklyn wearing the MA hood shows it to be more a deep turquoise (Figure 16),[51] and doctors have maroon hoods fully lined with faculty colour. The faculty colours are:

---

ment/graduates/hoods-and-colours.html (accessed 28 April 2021). Malaya does not have a comparable webpage.

[50] Haycraft, *Degrees and Hoods (1972)*, page 103. Oddly, there appears to be nothing about it in *Academical Dress*.

[51] Both Singapore and Malaya use a dark blue.

Arts light cerise

Laws medium blue (the same as used for the London Law degrees)

Medicine crimson

Pharmacy lilac

Dental Surgery russet brown

Engineering deep orange

Science gold

Philosophy light green

Education white

These were to be repeated at Southampton, with the exception of Philosophy, and to a lesser extent at Hull. But there are anomalies: the BEd and MEd do not wear the logical hoods of blue lined with white, but wear the BA and MA hoods with a white binding on the cowl, and the PhD has a hood lined with green and bound on all edges with faculty colour.[52] The scheme 'enables every graduate whatever the Faculty to have a hood fully lined with silk, avoids, edging of hoods (apart from Education and Philosophy)', but he does not say why these needless exceptions exist. But as London had added faculty bindings to the already distinctive Philosophy claret silk, this may be behind that decision. He notes that the neckbands are not edged, are cut on the curve, and are not let in. The entry in Degrees and Hoods ends: 'Other universities should take note of this achievement'.

The University of Southampton

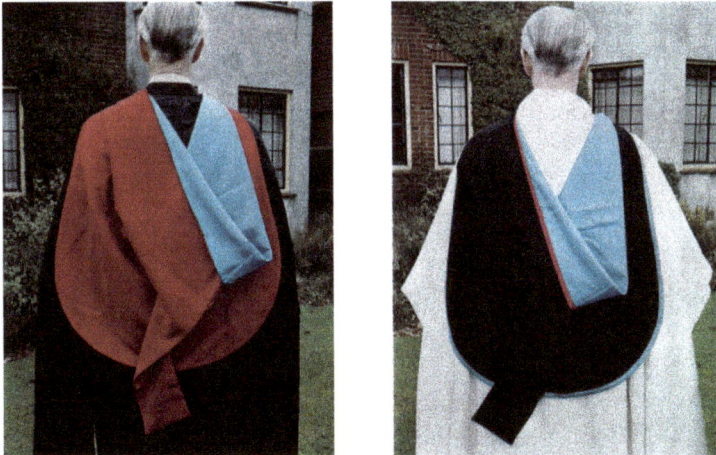

Figure 18: Franklyn wearing the Southampton doctors' and MA hoods

No study of Franklyn's involvement at Southampton has yet been undertaken, but we can pick up from correspondence between other universities that it was less than smooth. The scheme follows the 'Franklyn system' to the letter: bachelors in London BA gown and Burgon hood; masters in Oxford MA gown

---

[52] There was no MPhil or BPhil, though they would be easily enough slotted into the scheme.

and London hood; and doctors in Oxford robe and hood. All hoods are lined with a university silk (in this case, peacock blue), and bordered (except for doctors) with faculty colour; the gowns and robes have faculty colour cords and buttons on the yokes, and on the sleeves of the bachelors' gowns also.[53]

The faculty colours of the original scheme are:[54]

Arts cerise	**Medicine** crimson
Education white	('provided for' in 1967)
Engineering orange	**Science** rich gold
Laws blue – same as the 'university silk'	**Social Science** light green

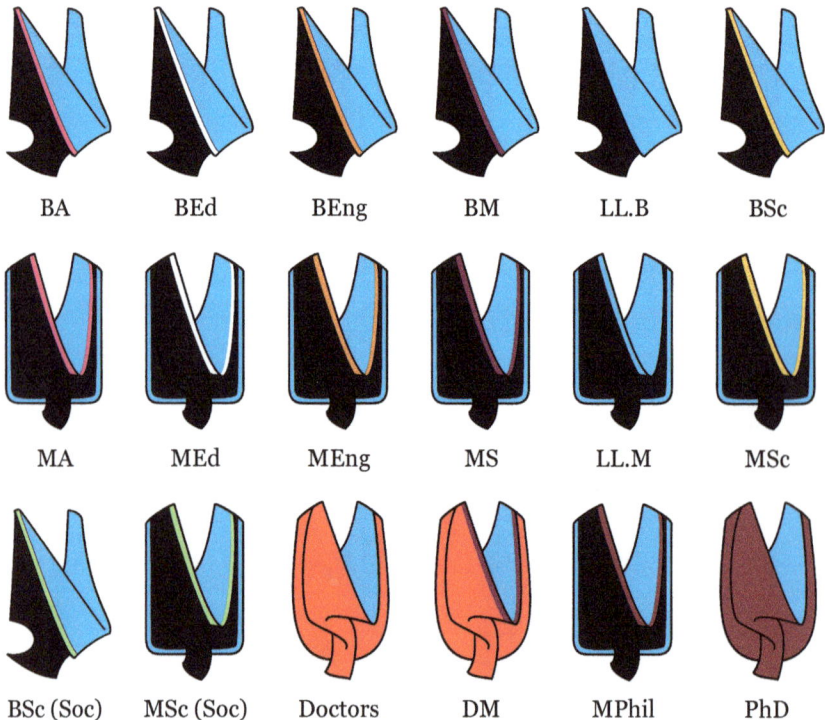

Figure 19: Hoods of the University of Southampton

The weakness is the Laws colour. As it is the same as the lining, the LL.B and LL.M hoods are made with the lining bound over. One has to wonder why a

---

[53]The cords were changed to become blue on all gowns in 1993, with those on the PhD and higher doctors becoming claret and scarlet respectively.

[54]The other faculty colours postdate Franklyn, and it is assumed these are the suggestions of the robemakers.

different shade of blue was not chosen.[55] There is also the peculiarity that none of the doctors' hoods are bound with faculty colour, so (as Franklyn had testily remarked about the pre-1934 Cambridge scheme) 'one hood did duty' for DLitt, DSc, LL.D, etc. The logic for this seems to be expressed by Franklyn in a letter to the Registrar of Hull:

> Doctors' hoods need not be edged because the cord and button on the gown would be the faculty colour as would the cord and tassel on the round velvet cap.[56]

Leaving aside the cords on the bonnet, we may ask why, in that case, the bachelors' and masters' hoods needed to be edged, as their gowns also had coloured cords and buttons – though of course those on the yokes of the gowns are hidden by the hood when in use in any case.

The University of Hull

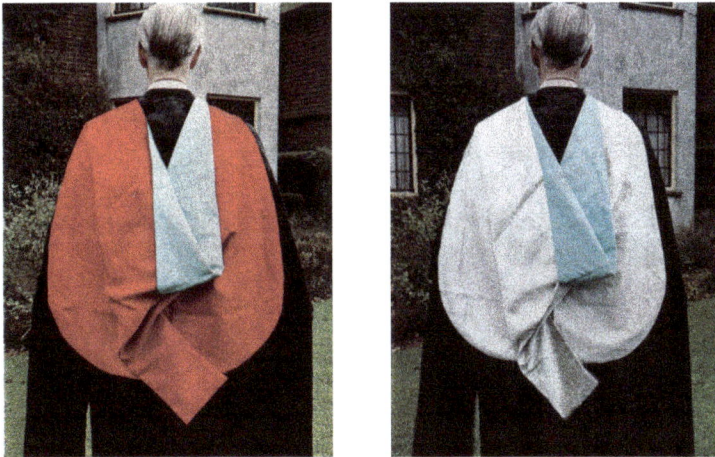

Figure 20: Franklyn wearing the Hull higher doctors' and DMus hoods

The story of Hull's designs have been covered in Dr Richard Baker's article in TBS 11.[57] Franklyn wrote to University College, Hull, on 12 November, 1953, offering his services should the College gain a charter, and, as ever, started to act as if he had already been accepted: the initial letter lays out principles and raises questions that would have been more appropriate at a later stage.

---

[55] Powder blue was later chosen as the colour for Nursing: doubtless this would not have pleased Franklyn, as he would most likely have wanted a shade of crimson to align with Medicine.

[56] Franklyn to Hull, 12 November 1953, quoted in Baker, 'The Academic Dress of the University of Hull', and most of what follows is taken from that source.

[57] Ibid., page 31. This survey does not take notice of later developments and additions to the scheme, for which see Dr Baker's article. The correspondence between Franklyn and Wippell is held in the Burgon Society archive: a handlist is available online: https://www.burgon.org.uk/wp-content/uploads/Burgon-Society-JWippell-re-Hull.pdf .

The upshot was, as we have seen, that the Registrar contacted his opposite number at Southampton, and was duly warned.[58]

He proposed a similar system to Southampton's, all hoods being lined with a single 'university' silk, with the usual progression Burgon [s2] → London [f3] → Oxford full [f5]. The gowns followed suit, with the progression London BA [b4] → Oxford MA [m1] → Oxford doctor [d2], with cords and buttons of faculty colour. The sole difference is that the Hull hoods are not bound with faculty colour.

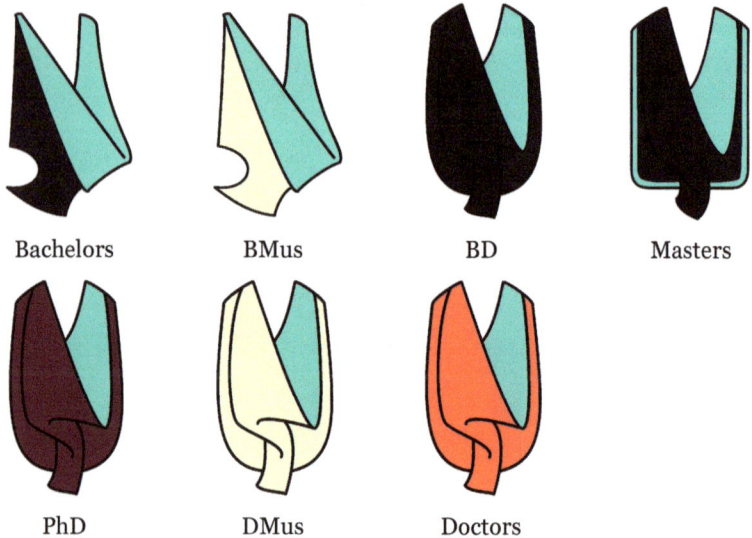

Bachelors	BMus	BD	Masters
PhD	DMus	Doctors	

Figure 21: Hoods of the University of Hull

His original suggestion for the 'university silk' was a rich orange shade, which he had specified for Engineering at Southampton, with a possible alternative of cerise. But the relevant committee wanted a shade of blue, ruled out orange at once, and would consider cerise if no suitable shade of blue could be found. Eventually the well-known turquoise was settled on.

The faculty colours are less than happy. They appeared as cords and buttons on the sleeves of the bachelors gowns, and on the yokes of all gowns and dress robes, with the exception of Music. Arts was given silver,[59] Economic Science grey, Music cream, and Education, a later addition, had white. All of these, after some degree of use, become indistinguishable. For some reason, Franklyn decided to separate Music out. The DMus was given a cream damask robe with turquoise facings and sleeves, and a hood of cream damask lined turquoise, which is in line with historic practice, and he gave it

---

[58] See above, page 16.

[59] Although silver was Hull's idea: it seems that Franklyn's suggestion was pink, as at Southampton, but Hull thought it was 'a bit noticeable'. Baker, 'The Academic Dress of the University of Hull', page 39.

the Oxford gimp gown for undress. But he also gave that gown to the BMus: and if so, why not to the LL.B, BSc, etc? He also gave it a hood of cream damask lined turquoise, but of the Burgon shape. This is a total innovation, as the damask shell is proper to the DMus,[60] and it is not clear what his thinking was on this.

The other exception was the BD, which was given a black cloth hood of Oxford full shape, lined with turquoise, and a master's gown. This at least does follow the Oxford precedent, though the coloured lining, as opposed to black, is new.

What he seems to have done is to conflate the Oxford and London schemes, with a good deal of his own invention. Southampton, when it was set up, had no Faculties of Music or Divinity, so those exceptions did not arise there.[61]

The Australian National University

This was established in 1951 as a postgraduate university and had Franklyn robes: this was at the request of the Council of the university, but it is as yet not clear how he came by the commission. The hoods were to be as follows:

> **Masters** of the 'improved' London shape, black cloth lined
> peacock blue shot green;
> **PhD** of the Cambridge shape, blue silk, lined peacock blue
> shot green;
> **Other Doctors** of the Cambridge shape, scarlet cloth lined
> peacock blue shot green.[62]

Although as proposed, all hoods were to be 'precisely as the pattern of the Oxford doctors'. The shot silk (which would appear to be lighter in shade than the Wales Arts mazarin blue shot green) could in the end not be used, owing to import restrictions, and so a blue corded silk was substituted.[63] Faculty colours are given, but it is not clear where they were to be used: there seems to be no provision for them to be used on the hoods: possibly as cords and buttons on the gowns.[64]

In due course, the University established bachelors' degrees. He remarks:

> Later, the University decided to confer Bachelors' degrees as
> well, but the designer of the original complete System of Aca-
> demical Dress was not informed and he was not consulted.[65]

---

[60] Indeed, if both hoods are made in the Warham shape [f11], they are identical.
[61] It granted the BA in Music. The BMus was a much later addition.
[62] Haycraft, *Degrees and Hoods (1972)*, page 62.
[63] Initially a blue cloth made from Australian wool.
[64] The faculty colours are: Arts: blue; Laws: purple; Science: green; Oriental Studies: blue bordered 1" terra-cotta; Economics: gold.
[65] Haycraft, *Degrees and Hoods (1972)*, page 160. The use of the third person to refer to himself is interesting.

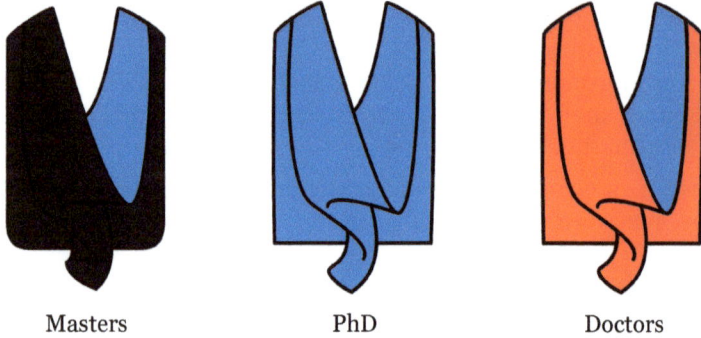

Masters   PhD   Doctors

Figure 22: Australian National University original hoods

The later hoods, which as we may expect, are 'grossly inferior and ... not distinctive', were as follows:

> **Bachelors** of the Burgon shape, black bordered four inches faculty colour;
> **Masters** of the Burgon shape, black lined faculty colour;
> **PhD** of the Cambridge shape, blue silk, lined self-colour;
> **Higher Doctors** of the Cambridge shape, scarlet cloth lined faculty colour.[66]

The gowns that go with these hoods are:

> **Bachelors** the Cambridge BA gown in black [b2];
> **Masters** the Oxford MA gown in black [m1];
> **PhD** as for masters, with blue facings;
> **Higher Doctors** of the Oxford pattern [d2] shape, scarlet cloth faced with faculty colour.[67]

Smith makes no reference to the original scheme. Given Franklyn's preferences, it is entirely probable that masters wore the Oxford MA gown, and doctors a scarlet Oxford gown, with blue facings. It would seem extremely unlikely that he gave the PhD the faced MA gown – his usual provision was a doctoral gown in crimson – and one would expect the London BA [b4] for the bachelors.

It is perhaps telling that Franklyn lists his unaltered scheme in the main body of *Degrees and Hoods*, (indeed, as a reproduction of Statute No 17, with the Registrar's name attached), while the revised scheme, which had been in use for some time, is relegated to a 'Supplementary Note' in the Addenda. Doubtless the distance of several thousand miles gave the University the courage to ignore him.

---

[66] Haycraft, *Degrees and Hoods (1972)*, page 160.
[67] Hugh Smith and Kevin Sheard, *Academic Dress and Insignia of the World*, A A Balkema, Cape Town (1970), volume 1, page 81.

Revisions to existing schemes

In addition to his own schemes, Franklyn was active in suggesting revisions to existing ones. Of these, the best-known is his interference at Cambridge in 1934. These reforms, instigated by the University itself, brought some order to what had become a rather incoherent system.[68] Franklyn's correspondence with the University is published in his *Academical Dress* of 1970.[69] As so often with Franklyn, his prejudices and preconceptions are allowed to influence his thinking, and his lack of grasp of historical principles (at least when it suited his case) is astonishing. This is particularly plain on page 176, when he fulminates about the MusM, MSc, MLitt, and LL.M all wearing the MA hood. He seems not to have understood that they wore this in virtue of their standing as MAs: 'Thus, one hood, the MA, did duty for MA, LL.M, MusM, MLitt, MSc, etc., a truly amazing state of affairs!' The MLitt and MSc did not in fact wear the black *silk* hood of an MA, but a black *cloth* one, with the white silk lining, which had appeared with these degrees in 1920. So it was not the same hood. It is interesting to note that, twenty years later, he caused precisely the same to happen at Hull, where all the masters use the same hood, of black silk lined with turquoise silk.

The 1933 Reports of the Council acknowledged the receipt of 'certain criticisms', without specifying their source, and said they had been 'carefully considered', but that they did not see their way to modifying their proposals, 'save in two matters'. These were that bachelors should have a hood of faculty silk, lined and bound with fur after the style of the BA. This appears to have been initiated by the Faculty of Music, which stated that the MusB hood (dark cherry satin lined and bound fur) was 'perhaps the most beautiful of all academic decorations', and I think we may hear Franklyn speaking here, despite the acknowledged source; thus the LL.B and MB hoods were to be brought into line with it. This was a pity, as it would have enabled an easy distinction between baccalaureates which ranked above the BA with the originally proposed hoods (black lined faculty colour, the cape edged fur), and those which ranked below it (faculty colour, half-lined and bound fur).[70] The other matter was that there were minor revisions to the sleeve-decorations of some of the gowns.

He later attempted the same thing at Oxford while he was resident at Exeter College for his abandoned DPhil, but with a total lack of success – possibly because he suggested the reforms, and not the University.[71] In 1941 he wrote

---

[68]See further, Nicholas Groves, 'The Academic Robes of Graduates of the University of Cambridge from the End of the Eighteenth Century to the Present Day', *Transactions of the Burgon Society* 13 (2013) 74–100.

[69]Charles A H Franklyn, *Academical Dress from the Middle Ages to the Present Day, including Lambeth Degrees*, W E Baxter Ltd, Lewes, Sussex (1970), pages 176–198.

[70]This would thus have solved the problem the EdB and BTh, being respectively light blue silk half-lined and bound fur, and either black silk or, more likely, dove shot silk, half-lined and bound fur. The MusB at that time ranked below the BA.

[71]I am grateful to Dr Andrew North for this information.

to the Vice-Chancellor, urging him to initiate a reform of the robes to make them more 'historically accurate'. Franklyn wanted a special committee set up, on which of course he would serve, assisted by certain other experts. (In connexion with this, he wrote a number of letters saying that, in order to serve on the committee, he would have to be made an MA of the University. It did not happen.) He was fairly easily kept at arm's length by the University, as of course the country was in the middle of a war (although Franklyn continued to write asking when the committee was to be set up), but once the war was over, a new Vice-Chancellor was in office, who was not at all interested in the matter. Franklyn's 'Brief Statement' is reproduced in full on pages 166–171 of *Academical Dress*, dated '30 January '41 (revised 7 March '41).' He gives the Commentary on the Memorandum – in fact, the reply by Strickland Gibson, Sub-Librarian at the Bodleian Library on page 172. Gibson's handling of him is masterly:

> Cambridge fortunately reformed the dress of her alumni at a favourable time. Oxford may not be able to proceed on quite the same lines. There is a prohibition in the Laudian Code that members of the University should in the matter of academical dress abstain from imitating anything that tends to luxury and pride. Silk is now and may remain an article of luxury. The maintenance of a colour standard has presented difficulties for some years past. A complete DLitt outfit costs about £30, but already, I hear, only second-hand robes are available. If Oxford has to discard silk gowns and robes (Convocations habits too might have to go) differentiation could still satisfactorily be obtained by designing three or four kinds of black gowns (some with distinctive facings) with hoods in variety to indicate the different degrees. As it is quite possible that after the war efforts will be made to reduce University expenses still further it would be helpful if an alternative scheme were put forward on these lines. Differentiation can be bought at too high a price. The robe of a Doctor of Music must be very expensive. After all it's not the robe he wears but the tune he whistles that matters.[72]

Franklyn's comments on this show that he has absolutely no sense of the delicate irony with which Gibson writes, but takes it as encouragement, and makes several points which he claims are founded on Gibson's remarks, but are in fact not. Perhaps the most bizarre is his reaction to Gibson's saying that the DCL's colour was once violet, and perhaps this should be reinstated. No, says Franklyn: because it is 'the colour of the Faculty of Medicine *in London*' (my italics).[73]

---

[72] Franklyn, *Academical Dress*, pages 172–173.
[73] And of course the Bristol PhD, a scarlet Oxford robe with violet sleeves and facings, had been in use for some time.

The issue was effectively shelved in 1948, by relegating the question of the committee to 'business pending'. Despite this, Franklyn attempted to keep the issue live by bombarding the University with letters on the subject. It was finally laid to rest on 18 October 1954, when the Hebdomadal Council voted eleven to five 'not to revive the question of the reform of academic dress'. Franklyn's footnote on page 171 reads: 'Note: Nothing was done, but in 1958 a federation of tailors told the University what they proposed to make for graduates!' This was in fact the register of colours and materials drawn up by the Oxford Federation of Merchant Tailors, and approved by the University on 12 February 1957, with copies held by the University and the Federation.[74]

This episode casts another interesting light on Franklyn. Once he had suggested the committee to the University, it then became for him a question of when it was to be set up, ignoring the intermediate stage of *if* it was to be set up.

Had his Oxford reforms been taken seriously, far from being more 'historically accurate', they would have introduced all manner of novelties. They centred round his obsession with faculty colours, and, as so often, reveal a total lack (or wilful disregard) of knowledge of the history he claims to be promoting. (One wonders what his DPhil thesis might have been like.) He was particularly offended by the fact that the DM and DCL share a robe and hood, as do the DLitt and DSc. Likewise, the BM and BCL use the same hood, as did the BLitt and BSc.[75] Had he had his way, the civil lawyers would have had mid-blue as their 'faculty colour', the medics crimson, the scientists grey, musicians pink, and the graduates in letters pale blue, the divines keeping the black they already had (see Figure 23 and Table 1).

He omits the BPhil from his list, as it was not introduced until 1946. He also refuses to allow what he calls the 'Junior Division' to have the Oxford plain shape [s1] – it *must* be Burgon.[76] It is unclear why, having cut a swathe through the historical robes of Oxford, he balked at changing the BMus from 'purple' (actually, lilac) to the logical pink – he notes it 'should really be of corded silk or satin of the same shade of pink as [is] used to line the DMus hood'.

On the other hand, he quite rightly says that

> The DPhil student, if not a graduate of Oxford, at present wears a Commoners' gown of length reaching to the knee.[77] In

---

[74]And yet in 1970, in *Academical Dress* (page 102) we find him opining about Oxford, that 'The colour for each degree should be fixed, sealed patterns should be held in the University office ...' – although given the nature of the book, it is hard to know quite when that was written.

[75]And their replacements, the MLitt and MSc also share a hood.

[76]He says in a footnote: 'Named after the Very Rev John Burgon, MA, DD, sometime Dean of Christ Church'. Burgon was, of course Dean of Chichester, and was MA and BD: he never proceeded to the DD. His colleges were Worcester and Oriel. This careless approach to factual accuracy (odd – and possibly worrying – in a medical man) may partially explain the abandoned BLitt/DPhil.

[77]Now called the Graduate Student's gown.

as much as the Commoners' gown is by Statute of full length (*Toga talaris*), the DPhil students' gown is something less than a Commoner's.[78]

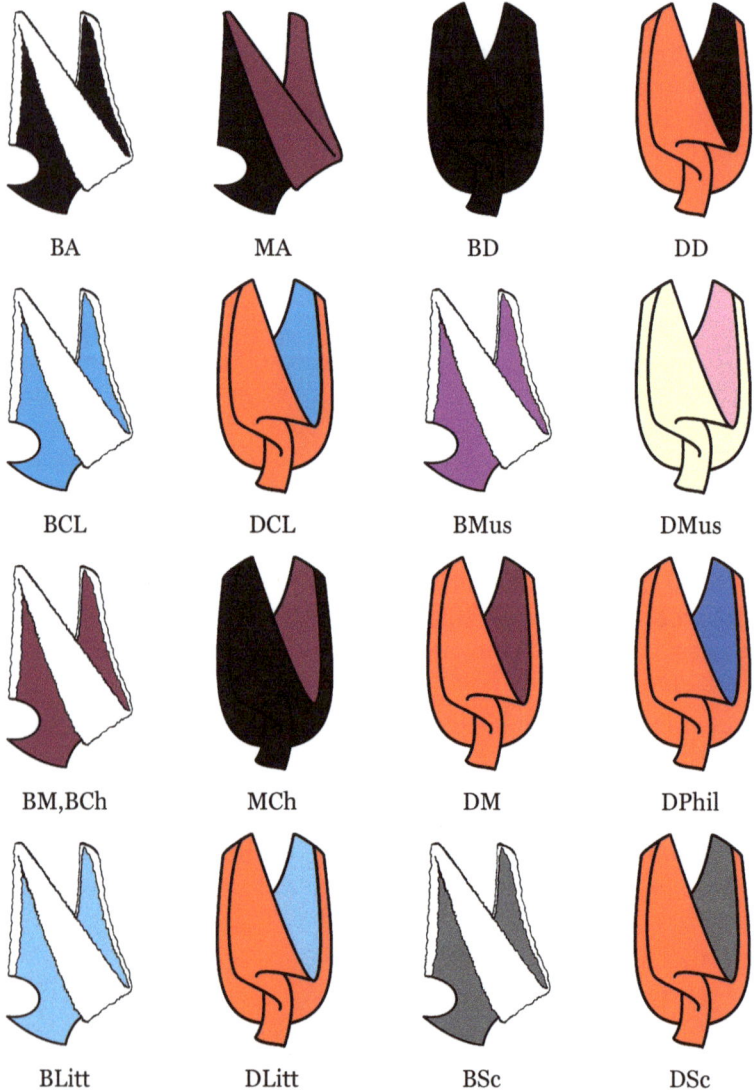

BA	MA	BD	DD
BCL	DCL	BMus	DMus
BM,BCh	MCh	DM	DPhil
BLitt	DLitt	BSc	DSc

Figure 23: Franklyn's proposed Oxford hoods

He goes on to suggest that all non-Oxford graduates, whether reading for the DPhil or any other degree, should be allowed to wear the old SCL gown – i.e., the flap-collar gown used for BCL, etc, without any gimp trimming.

---

[78] Franklyn, *Academical Dress*, page 170.

Degree	Franklyn's proposed hood (and doctoral robe)
BA	[s2] black silk and fur
MA	[s2] black silk and (shot) crimson silk
BD	[f5] black silk lined black silk
DD	[f5] scarlet cloth lined black silk (velvet on robe)
BCL	[s2] mid-blue silk and fur
DCL	[f5] scarlet cloth lined mid-blue silk
BM,BCh	[s2] crimson silk and fur
MCh	[f5] black silk and (shot) crimson silk
DM	[f5] scarlet cloth lined (shot) crimson silk
BMus	[s2] purple silk and fur (but 'should really be' pink)
DMus	[f5] cream brocade lined pink silk.
BLitt	[s2] light blue silk and fur
DLitt	[f5] scarlet cloth lined light blue silk
BSc	[s2] grey silk and fur
DSc	[f5] scarlet cloth lined grey silk
DPhil	[f5] scarlet cloth lined dark blue silk

Table 1: Franklyn's proposed Oxford amendments.[79]

This probably would have been a good move, as he has demonstrated that the 'advanced/graduate students' gown' is based on a mistake.[80] Of course, we can now know that this was the (former) DPhil student speaking. Indeed, until 1957, all students, regardless of what degree they were studying for, were lumped together as 'Commoners', unless they held an Oxford degree. (From 1957 they became 'Other members receiving tuition or supervision' in the College lists.)

Failed attempts

It has long been thought that Franklyn attempted to get himself appointed to the other 1960s universities, and evidence of this is coming to light.

---

[79] Reworked from his list in *Academical Dress*, p 164.
[80] The commoners' gown was indeed made full-length until well into the nineteenth century, but it became the fashion for freshmen to 'distress' their gowns so that they would look less new, and thus appear to be of a more senior standing. The robemakers then started to make the gowns shorter and shorter in the first place, until they reached the exiguous length familiar today. It would be interesting to see what a Proctor would say to a commoner who arrayed himself in a gown of statutory length. These days, non-Oxford graduates reading for any higher degree (though not for the BA) may wear the robes of their own university instead of the advanced students' gown.

The University of Exeter

Franklyn sent a 'Preliminary Memorandum' to University College, Exeter, in 1955,[81] but he was not asked to design for them.

The University of Sussex

This is possibly the best-known of his failed attempts, of which he says

> The academical dress adopted for this university is, perhaps, the most deplorable, freakish, and unorthodox of any British University ... This present system is a calamity because the writer could have given to Sussex the most beautiful robes of all, reminiscent of the blue-green of the sea and the green of the Downs.[82]

The 'blue-green of the sea' might imply the blue-green shot silk which was proposed for the ANU.

Owing to Malcolm Kemp's work on Sussex,[83] a version of the scheme has come to light, though it was a joint effort with George Shaw. The scheme was submitted by Shaw alone,[84] and he says it is 'a modified version of my original scheme'. It is as follows:

Gowns

Undergraduates A Sussex blue gown of Durham undergraduate pattern [u4] – i.e., Oxford scholar with a 6" slit in the forearm seam.

Bachelors A black gown of Oxford BA pattern [b8], with sleeves reaching the hem. The bottom 6" of the forearm seam are left open, and there is a black button at the top of the slit.

Masters A black gown of basic pattern [m10], the inner edge cut at an acute angle, with an inverted-T armhole, with a black button at the top of the upright cut.

Doctors undress As for masters, with the addition of a flap collar. There is a row of Cambridge lace round the armholes, and for higher doctors, along the outer edge of the facings also.

Doctors dress Of the Cambridge pattern [d1], in claret for PhD, and scarlet for others, the sleeves lined and the facings covered with Sussex blue. There is 1" of faculty colour along the edge of the facings, and a cord and button of faculty colour on each sleeve.

---

[81]Referred to in letter, Franklyn to AG Knott, 20 February 1955; BS Archive, U/Hull/A/64.
[82]Franklyn, *Academical Dress*, page 208.
[83]FBS dissertation.
[84]Letter from Shaw to John (later Lord) Fulton, 18 February 1961, sent from Lancing.

Hoods

Bachelors Of the Burgon shape [s2], in Sussex blue, lined with the faculty colour and 'edged' with white fur. 'The neckband to be V-shaped and with a loop to hold it.'

Masters Of the London shape [f3], in Sussex blue, lined and bound on the cape for 0.5" with faculty colour. Neckband as for bachelors.

Doctors Of the Oxford full shape [f5], in claret for PhD, and scarlet for others, lined with Sussex blue, and bound on the cowl 0.5" in and out with faculty colour. (Nothing specified for the neckband.)

Hats All bachelors and masters were to wear the black cloth square cap, doctors in undress a black velvet one, and in dress a black velvet bonnet with cords and tassels of faculty colour.

The bachelors' and masters' gowns turn up in Shaw's later scheme for Bath. The use of the Cambridge doctoral robe is interesting, as both Shaw and Franklyn tended to use the Oxford pattern, though the design, with faculty edgings, parallels the London PhD.

The hoods have Franklyn's fingerprints all over them. There is the progression in shapes from bachelor [s2] to master [f3] to doctor [f5]. There is the use of blue as a university colour. What is unusual is the use of the university blue for the shells of the masters' and bachelors' hoods, and also the addition of fur, which he is not known to have used anywhere else. Was it at the request of the University – or was the scheme unsolicited? The exact manner of 'edging' the hood is not made clear, but this was a binding of one inch on the cowl edge. The faculty colours are those of Southampton – Arts was neyron rose (Southampton: cerise) and Science deep gold (Southampton: rich gold).[85] These are given BCC numbers – but the 'Sussex blue' is not. However, a prototype BSc hood was given to John Balsdon, and it is made in a mid-blue (see Figure 24).

The 'Independent University'

The correct name for this was University College, Buckingham – since 1983, the University of Buckingham. Founded in 1973, it could not award degrees, and did not avail itself of London external degrees: it awarded a Licence, designated LUCB, with a hood of Edinburgh shape [s4] in royal blue, lined white, worn with a London BA gown.

---

[85] Sussex had just the two faculties at the start, and awarded only BA, BSc, MA, and MSc. It is organized in Schools of Study, so the BA can be taken in several Schools. Thus a scheme with hoods dependent on the degree title makes sense. The colours are thus not 'faculty colours' *strictu sensu*, but 'degree colours'.

Figure 24: Prototype Sussex BSc hood

Franklyn got wind of it ('announced in the 'TIMES' in Thursday 12 November 1970'), and immediately designed a set of robes for it, and published them in the 1972 edition of *Degrees and Hoods* – listing it as The Independent University, between Hull and Kent.[86] He does say 'should this University materialise', and goes on to say that 'the undermentioned system is suggested which would ensure beauty, dignity, and distinction'. It lists only the hoods, of course, but as ever, we may assume that bachelors were to have the London BA gown [b4], masters the Oxford MA [m1], and doctors a robe of Oxford pattern [d2], with facings and sleeves of faculty colour.

All hoods were to be of the 'improved' Oxford full shape [f5], bachelors in black poplin, rayon, or silk lined with faculty colour; masters in dark blue poplin, rayon, or silk, lined with faculty colour; and doctors in scarlet cloth lined with faculty colour, but the PhD to have a hood a deep cherry cloth lined green, with the cowl edged with faculty colour for three-eighths of an inch. The faculty (more accurately, school) colours would be:

> **Language and Literature** pink
> **History and Government** light grey
> **Laws** blue
> **Biological sciences** old gold
> **Physical sciences** light gold
> **Philosophy** green

These are in line with what we would expect. Quite why the PhD needs a faculty border, when green is its unique marker, is unclear.

He also gives a list of degrees to be awarded: BA, MA, DLitt; LL.B. LL.M, LL.D; BSc, MSc, DSc; BSc(Econ), MSc(Econ), DSc(Econ); PhD: presumably

---

[86] Haycraft, *Degrees and Hoods (1972)*, page 11.

these, and the School structure, were in the original announcement in The Times.[87]

This scheme was not adopted (did they even know of it?), and the University based its scheme on the old LUCB hood, with faculty colour borders. It does use pink for Arts, and gold is assigned to the BSc(Econ), etc. But Laws is scarlet, and Science is maroon.

The University of Essex

This was a commission which he was gravely offended not to have gained, given his Essex ancestry. The correspondence is preserved in the archive at Essex.[88] Alas, it reveals nothing about any notional scheme, though he does imply that he had already designed one, but it does illustrate how he went to work – and what happened when he was turned down.

It starts with a letter of 21 September 1963 from Charles Leatherland to the Vice-Chancellor. The VC had told Franklyn that the question of academic dress was 'under discussion', but in response to Leatherland's formal acknowledgement, Franklyn wrote a long reply, which he was forwarding to the VC. Leatherland remarked perceptively:

> He seems to be a tiresome old gentleman. I have not acknowledged this letter, and I don't want to get involved in correspondence with him.

The next is a letter from Franklyn to the Vice-Chancellor, Albert Sloman, 3 December 1963. It is worth quoting in full:

> I feel compelled to write to you now because I am becoming more and more puzzled and alarmed. Years ago, the moment that a University of Essex was announced, I placed myself (?)unreservedly at the disposal of the promotion committee and of those who would form the nucleus at Hd.Qrs., & I offered to help design the most beautiful, dignified, and distinct academical and official Dress for the new University. I have had charming letters from several individuals, but NIL constructive, NIL definite, and no word of encouragement to go ahead.
>
> I am sure there is no other Essex-born man who is an expert on the subject and who has devoted a lifetime to it, & has designed complete systems for 4 or 5 of the British universities. It is quite beyond the capacity of tailors & robemakers. Finally, no new university would dream of designing ac: dress until

---

[87]Throughout his writings, the title of this publication, clearly the only newspaper he read, is invariably written in capitals.

[88]I am very grateful to the Revd Edmund Eggleston for providing copies of it. These are not numbered, so I simply use the internal dating.

a Charter had been issued, but now some of these embryo universities have started on robes when a charter was not even in draft! I would be very shocked if someone else, a non-Essex-born man, were asked to do this without any capable experience and knowledge.

In my experience, the normal procedure is for a sub-Committee of the Senate or Council to be appointed to consider reflect & advise on the matter of ac: dress, & it is usual for the V-C to be chairman of it. May I ask, please, has such a sub-Comt[ee] been appointed and are you its Chairman?

My mother's people have a continuous Essex descent from 1650 & my father was born at Ingatestone in 1868, & I was at Brentwood in 1896 (see Who's Who). Recently, some other universities have got into an awful mess through (?)using no expert help & have infringed the degrees of other universities. I look forward to a kind and encouraging letter from you.

[*written sideways along the last sheet*] PS I assume you are a cousin of HMP Sloman, MC, MA, Head of T[onbridge] S[chool] 1923–39?

This elicited a very short response on 10 December, addressed to 'Mr CAH Franklyn, MA, MD, FLS', saying that the Council of the University had 'made an appointment of a person to design its academic dress', and there would be a public announcement 'in due course'.

This prompted another response to Sloman on 11 December. It is headed 'Academic̲al Dress', even now instructing them on what he felt was the correct form of the word.

Thank you for you letter of yesterday, which gave me a nasty shock, for it is nasty for an Essex-born man, and a 300 years' connection with the county to be turned down flat and snubbed: and, presumably, a non-Essex-born man with no connection with the County asked to do this for you.

(2) Does this mean that I am (?)barred[89] out and am forbidden to show you the most beautiful and dignified system of Academic̲al Dress that I have got for you?[90]

(3) As your public announcement may not be in the TIMES, please be so good as to send me a copy of it, or otherwise I shall not see it.

(4) I assume that you are a life member of the Oxford Society. On Saturday you received the Dec: issue of OXFORD. If you have not thrown it out would you be so good as to read pp

---

[89] Possibly 'banned'.
[90] This implies he had jumped the gun and designed a set. No vestige of it has come to light.

102–06 – and see what my review says.

(5) I am not 'Mr'! I am a physician and specifically MB & MD
= Doctor <u>in</u> Medicine.

He then wrote again to Leatherland on 13 December, asking if he knew what
had happened: 'I have been spurned and pushed aside as of no value at
all!'. He refers to the 'curt note' from Sloman about the appointment, and
rehearses much of what he said to Sloman. He assumed that Leatherland
was not present 'when this decision was made'. He went on,

> Even now it is not too late for you can say it would be much to
> the advantage of the new university if we hear what Dr Charles
> Franklyn has to say, & we see *his* proposals before we commit
> ourselves.

The note of pathos did not work: Leatherland simply sent it on to the Vice-
Chancellor on 18 December with a covering note: 'another letter from this
troublesome old gentleman'. He did not think it needed any further action,
and could be archived. He said had responded briefly, expressing sorrow at
his disappointment, that he was not overlooked, and that the chosen designer
was an Essex man. Sloman replied 'I am afraid he is pestering me so much
that I now write only the shortest of notes to him'.

A further short (curt?) note from Sloman on 7 January 1964 informed
Franklyn that the designer chosen was Hardy Amies.

The final item is a letter of 13 January 1964 from Franklyn to the Secretary,
Miss Dawson:

> Many thanks indeed for your letter of the 10th an enclosure re
> academic<u>al</u> and official dress, received at 9.53 a.m. today. [Cor-
> rect spelling is academic<u>al</u> – refer to *several illegible words*][91]

> I am glad that the V-C had read the review in OXFORD Dec,
> issue.

> My colleague, Dr George W Shaw, MSc, DPhil, Director of
> the Dept of Biology at Lancing, a great authority on hoods &
> robes, whom I have been helping for years, and I, think it is
> fantastic to ask a ladies' dress maker to design ac: and official
> robes! And the fact that he has had to go to Ede & R for help
> makes it even more absurd. This means that John F Austin
> (one of Ede & R's directors) will virtually control, make, and
> (?)run everything. You will have to pay a big fee to <u>Edwin</u>
> Hardy Amies,[92] when you could have had the best scheme in

---

[91] The words in square brackets are written at the end of line, and shown by a caret mark as to
be inserted after 'academical'

[92] According to the Wikipedia article on him, he was born Edwin Amies, and adopted Hardy, his
mother's maiden name, during his teens, as it was her contacts in the fashion world that set
him on his path as a designer. Franklyn is being gratuitously rude. Amies was born in Maida
Vale, but attended Brentwood School, so the Essex connexion is tenuous. He was, of course,

the world designed by an expert for nix!

(2) I saw no report in TIMES. Was it in? As the Univ: of Essex has no Arms am I allowed to design these? This has been my work for 42 years.[93]

Written sideways along one side:

There is no such colour as Essex or (?)geranium red!

The Philosophical Society of England

This body was founded in 1913 by a group of amateur philosophers, concerned to provide an alternative to the formal university-based discipline, and awarded the diplomas of APhs and FPhS. The Fellowship had no fewer than six hoods in eighty years:

(a) 1913–25: Cambridge shape [f1], dark purple silk, lined blood red silk.

(b) 1925–39: Cambridge shape [f1], dark green, lined light green;

(c) 1939–46: Oxford simple shape [s1], dark green, lined pale green shot turquoise;

(d) 1946–48: London shape [f3], dark green, lined eau-de-nil;

(e) 1948–??: 'full or simple', dark green, lined and bound green shot blue – one in the Burgon Society's Collection is made in Oxford full shape [f5], and lined with Wales Arts silk.

(f) 19??–c1991: London shape [f3], dark green moiré, lined pale blue – this was the final hood.

Did Franklyn, who was a Fellow, design one or more of (c) to (e)? The use of the green shot blue silk may be indicative.[94] See Figure 25 for hood (e).

A life's work ...

Franklyn can be seen to have had a long career designing robes, and it is easy to trace his various trademarks in terms of patterns and colours emerging – and indeed it is just those trademarks that have made the identification of the hitherto unknown early schemes possible. Whether they are the most beautiful and dignified is, of course, a matter for the beholder, and maybe the wearer: their basic similarity makes such a judgment difficult. The four

---

far more than a 'ladies' dressmaker'. The statement about the fee was disingenuous: he was paid a substantial sum by Hull, and quite probably also by Southampton, Malaya, and ANU – and Malaya gave him an MA as well. Southampton told Hull he might expect an honorary degree - 'a mastership is sufficient' – but neither of them gave him one.

[93] He did not get this commission, either.

[94] Hood (f) is known to be the work of the late Dr Paul Faunch.

Figure 25: Fellowship hood of the Philosophical Society of England, 1948 version

universities are to be congratulated on getting workable schemes out of him that have worn well, and proved possible to adapt as need arose, though possibly not always in ways he would have approved.

Appendix 1: Comparative table of faculty colours in Franklyn's schemes

University	Arts	Divinity	Laws	Music	Letters	Science	Philosophy
Malaya 1949	cerise	—	blue	—	as Arts	gold	light green
Hull 1954	silver	scarlet	blue	cream	as Arts	gold	[claret][d]
Southampton 1952	cerise	—[f]	blue	ivory	as Arts	gold	[claret][d]
Sussex (unadopted)	neyron rose	—	—	—	—	gold	—
Ulster 1968	blue	—	—[e]	white	as Arts	green	gold
English Episcopal Church	red	purple[a]	blue[b]	pink	as Arts	—	light green
Western Orth Univ 1950	red	crimson	dark blue	lavender	old gold	violet	green
Western Int Univ 1952	crimson	scarlet	dark blue	lavender	old gold	—	green
Glastonbury 1951[c]	—	black	blue	cherry	crimson	grey	green
Intercollegiate[i]	?	crimson	blue[h]	gold	white	—	bronze green
Sulgrave 1942	?	?	?	lavender	old gold	—	crimson
'Franklyn's Own'[g]	[none]	black	mid-blue	pink	light blue	grey	green

Notes

a The BD was lined black.

b The EEC awarded degrees in both Laws (light blue) and Civil Law (dark blue).

c This conflates similar degrees using differing shades.

d The PhD and MPhil are awarded in all faculties, and Philosophy does not constitute a faculty in itself.

e Degrees in Laws use 'pale burgundy', but did not form part of the original Franklyn scheme.

f Degrees in Theology use violet, but did not form part of the original Franklyn scheme.

g These are what Franklyn conceived to be the historical English faculty colours, and to which he wished the Oxford scheme to be aligned. They are (with the exception of green for Philosophy) indeed extrapolated from the Oxonian scheme, but wrongly, as he did not (or refused to) understand the logic behind it.[95]

h Intercollegiate awarded degrees in both Laws (azure) and Civil Law (dark blue).

i This is the 1939 revision.

---

[95] See Alan J Ross, '*Togas gradui et facultati competentes*: The Creation of New Doctoral Robes at Oxford, 1895–1920', *Transactions of the Burgon Society* 10 (2010) 47–70.

Appendix 2: Original scheme for the Intercollegiate University

From Haycraft, *Degrees and Hoods*, 2nd edition, 1924.[96] Bachelors' hoods are 'simple shape', doctors' are 'full'. It is not clear what shape the MA had.

> **BA** sepia silk lined ivory satin
> **MA** black silk lined pale rose silk.
> **MusBac** sepia silk lined crimson silk.
> **MusDoc** scarlet cloth lined gold silk.
> **BD** violet silk lined ivory satin
> **DD** scarlet cloth lined crimson satin
> **LL.B** violet silk lined pale blue satin
> **LL.D** scarlet cloth lined pale blue satin
> **BLitt** sepia silk lined gold silk
> **DLitt** scarlet cloth lined white satin
> **BSc** violet silk lined gold silk
> **DSc** scarlet cloth lined violet satin
> **PhB** violet silk lined light green silk
> **PhD** scarlet cloth lined light green silk.

Appendix 3: Inter-College Relations

It is generally difficult to keep abreast with the highly fissiparous denominations outside the mainstream churches, and the same is true of the colleges associated with them, so it is hoped the following will make the relationships between the various bodies mentioned above clear.

As noted, Charles Leslie Saul set up the English Episcopal Church around 1944, changing its name first to the Protestant Evangelical Church of England, and then to the Protestant Episcopal Reformed Church in 1980. (A useful account of the church is to be found in Anson, *Bishops at Large*, page 231ff.) In conjunction with this, he set up Cranmer Hall Theological College to train aspirants to its ministry. The hoods were designed by Franklyn. On Saul's death in 1997, the college and church became independent of each other, and the college changed its name to avoid confusion with Cranmer Hall, which forms part of St John's College Durham, and became Cranmer Memorial Bible College and Seminary (CMBCS).

Saul also ran the London College of Theology, active in the 1940s and 1950s, again with a hood designed by Franklyn, awarded alike to Members (MLCT) and Fellows (FLCT): the right to wear it was gained purely by paying a subscription.

---

[96] Frank W Haycraft, *The Degrees and Hoods of the World's Universities & Colleges*, second edition, The Cheshunt Press, London and Cheshunt (1924), page 55.

At around the same time, the Evangelical Preachers' Association (EPA) was awarding a Fellowship (FEPA; hood: [f1], black, the cowl bound 1" red), and in 1958 it set up the Evangelical Institute of Theology, which awarded a Diploma (hood: [s1] navy blue, lined sky-blue). In 1978 this changed its name to the National College of Divinity (NCD), and then in 1986 to the International College of Divinity (ICD). (Meanwhile, the EPA changed its name to the Ministry of Evangelism, and later to the Fellowship of Evangelistic Ministries, which now runs the Evangelistic Academy.)

In 1986, the ICD and CMBCS merged, retaining the CMBCS name. The hoods currently used by CMBCS have no relation to any of the earlier ones, save the use of a grey lining.

6 Publications on Academic Dress

Franklyn produced one major work on academic dress, and was a co-editor of another, and these will be considered first. There are also various minor works.

Academical Dress from the Middle Ages to the Present Day, including Lambeth Degrees

Academical Dress was published privately in 1970, and 'is the result of many years' study of the subject'.[1] Franklyn was under no illusions about the seminal status of the work:

> I began the work at school in Sept. 1910 when 14, through my student days and it has been my lifelong interest since. Similar works are little more than lists which become out of date very quickly, or are wrong from the outset, and must be revised if they are to be of any use. There is not another work quite like mine in detail and I expect it shall become and remain the standard reference work on the subject for a very long time.[2]

Further praise was, we are told, forthcoming from a very august source:

> Bodley's Librarian sent me a letter of praise and said that I had produced much new and unknown material, and an Oxford Scholar (B.Litt, DPhil: Oxon), President & V-C of Windsor University Ontario and an Old Rhodes Scholar wrote to say it merited a D.Litt!![3]

---

[1] It is entirely possible that it was to be the basis of his projected DPhil thesis. The Prologue says on page vi: '... the writer devoted one academic year, October 1940 to June 1941, to research in the Bodleian Library, working under the direction of ... Dr Alfred B Emden'.

[2] Letter, Franklyn to Francis Steer, 22 December 1970, tipped into the copy currently owned by Dr Paul Coxon.

[3] Letter, Franklyn to Francis Steer, 22 December 1970, tipped into the copy currently owned by Dr Paul Coxon. This was John Francis Leddy, 1911–98, President and Vice-chancellor of Windsor University 1964–78. Maybe Leddy spoke with forked tongue: he did not see his way to causing Windsor to award Franklyn a DLitt. Interestingly, his successor as President in 1978 was a Mervyn Franklin (no relation so far as is known).

It starts with an oddity: the frontispiece is a black-and-white reproduction of the portrait of Sir Brian Tuke (1450–1545), who is, we are told, wearing 'typical Tudor pre-MA bag sleeves, worn by a non-academic personage'. Alas, as the portrait is half-length, the sleeves cannot be seen, merely the armhole, and the reproduction is so dark that it is hard to make out what exactly he is wearing in any case.[4] Why not have a picture of some form of academic dress? For such a visual subject, the lack of illustration is hard to understand. The chapter on 'The Hood' does have some line drawings, which are taken whole-sale from Herbert Norris' work *Costume and Fashion*, vol 1,[5] and he uses Norris' figure numbers, so that we proceed (for example, on pages 120–121) from figure 52, to figure 144, 163, 143, 164 – with page references to Norris' book.[6]

The list of contents on page v is of little use, as it is not paginated. There is no index, and the Bibliography is arranged alphabetically by title as far as item 41, is then added to at random, and does not distinguish between books and articles.

It is worth quoting the 'Author's Note: the scope of this work', as it sets out his stall:

> This work has been devoted to the Academical Dress of Grad-uates, and the comparatively modern ceremonial robes of cer-tain officers and dignitaries, such as Chancellor, Vice-Chancellor, Chairman of the Court, or of Convocation, Principal, and so on, have been omitted purposely (except from the University of London official list). These are for the most part modern, or in the Chancellor's case Stewart [sic] period onwards, and do not affect the developmental or evolutionary basis of our work: such robes are excrescences and without influence on the whole.
>
> Certain non-graduates' gowns at Oxford have been referred to where they have an important bearing on the whole or evolutionary scheme, or come into a critical analysis. The Cambridge college undergraduates' gowns have been omitted purposely and may be studied by anyone interested, in AG Almond's booklet: they are modern, dating from the period 1805–40.
>
> The Robes of the Oxford, Cambridge, and London Bedels or Bedells, as well as those of the Oxford and Cambridge Proctors, have been included for obvious reasons.[7]

Modern is as modern does, it would seem. If nineteenth-century undergrad-uate gowns, let alone a seventeenth-century Chancellor's robe, are modern,

---

[4]The sleeves of his doublet do look horribly like houndstooth check!
[5]Herbert Norris, *Costume and Fashion*, J M Dent and Sons (1947).
[6]It is good to note that these drawings were Norris' 'gift to the writer of this book in 1941'.
[7]Franklyn, *Academical Dress*, page vii.

and thus of no interest, we might wonder why the 1953 robes of Hull are not even more 'modern' or 'excrescences'.

Unfortunately, the material was not competently edited, and in places appears to be merely a transcription of his notebooks (do they still exist?): thus it contains as still current material that was long out-of-date in 1970. For example, Durham is castigated for awarding 'all kinds of queer degrees and diplomas, that are not really proper degrees at all, vidz, LTh, ASc, LSSc, BHy, DHy, DCh, etc'.[8] They were, he said, not 'normal-looking, or elegant', and he advised students to have nothing to do with them, but to 'take a real degree from another university'. But the LTh had been withdrawn in 1946, the ASc and LSSc were long-extinct by 1940, as were the Hygiene degrees. The DCh was transferred to Newcastle in 1963, but hardly, if ever, awarded. What is said to be Section 11 of Chapter III, 'Mural Tablets (deferred)', but is actually 'Section (xiv): I. Mural Tablets, Monuments, Stained Glass, and Statues', has a note: 'Owing to the War and consequent difficulties in travel, the increasingly critical period developing in 1941, and more pressing demand for medical services, this had be left over at any rate for the time being'. One does wonder quite which war was being fought in 1970, and what he had done in the meantime to gather this information. The date 1941 is notable: it is when he abandoned his research at Oxford to return to medical practice, which lends further weight to the idea that this book is based on that research.[9]

It also includes verbatim transcripts of articles taken from other writers; it is unclear if he had their permission. These form the bulk of the first nine chapters, some 200 pages out of 244 of text. Another example of the lack of attention to detail: Chapter III ('Academical Dress and Ecclesiastical Dress in the Middle Ages') starts with a summary of what is included in numbered sections, 1–13 (Arabic numerals). But the sections in the text are given Roman numerals, and bear no relation to the summary – what he says is section '5. Canons of the Church, Documents, and Statutes' turns out, once we find it, to be 'Section (ix)'.

In many places it is simply factually inaccurate, although this is usually in relation to universities in which he had no particular interest. This is not the place to give a full critique of the work, but some of his more glaring errors may give an idea of their nature. In Chapter XI, 'Other Universities),[10] he informs us that Liverpool uses hoods 'of the Oxford MA type' for bachelors and masters, and 'of the Cambridge MA type' for doctors: in fact, all three grades use an Edinburgh pattern hood.[11] Sheffield is told off for describing the doctors' hoods as 'red': 'No one knows why they use the word 'red', when

---

[8] Ibid., page 206.

[9] He makes much the same assertion on page 102 in relation to portraits.

[10] That is, not Oxford, Cambridge, or London, an attitude which pervades his outlook. He also refers to the various universities as 'she' or 'her': 'Sheffield has a system for her hoods'.

[11] Franklyn, *Academical Dress*, page 207. Admittedly, this shape did start life as the Oxford MA pattern current about 1860.

the word scarlet should be used to denote what is meant'[12] Actually, no: Sheffield has scarlet robes for its doctors, but the hoods they wear with them are in fact, and always have been, of a darker red silk. This reveals a basic flaw which runs through all his work: he had very fixed ideas on what ought to be, and was capable of writing in such as way as to imply that it was in fact so, as opposed what was actually the case. A careless reading of that sentence about Sheffield doctors, for example, would lead one to believe that it does indeed have scarlet hoods, laxly described as red. Another example of this is that he thought (probably rightly) that Birmingham's bachelors' hoods would be improved if they were lined white in addition to the faculty border (as at London), and thus he says they 'should' be so lined, which is ambiguous. Part of this may, of course, be blamed also on a lack of in-depth research (he relies almost exclusively on secondary sources), and as we have seen, a lack of rigour pervades his work even when the material is to hand:[13] in the days before the internet and freely available images, the number of Sheffield or Liverpool doctors he saw in their robes must have been few, if any, although anyone with a serious interest in the subject could be expected to have made themselves familiar with its finer points, especially as in 1970 there were only about twenty universities to worry about.

Another of his deathless remarks occurs under Sheffield:

> This modern [founded 1879, chartered 1905] University also grants degrees in Dental Surgery, Engineering, Technology, and Metallurgy. It would be interesting to know of anyone who has obtained one of these degrees has met with any success in life thereby![14]

One might be excused for retorting that perhaps dentists, engineers, and so forth, and indeed their clients, find them most useful.

Under Bristol, he opines that the system is 'so incomplete and the faculties are not manifest: the Regulations should be redrafted by an expert ...': one suspects that the only acceptable 'expert' would be Franklyn. Likewise he thinks that the Exeter 'Regulations are very sketchy, lax, and drawn up by non-experts' – as we have seen, he was rejected as Exeter's designer. Nottingham's robes 'are not too bad, and are not unorthodox' – but we learn that he 'had the privilege of contributing to this scheme before it was hatched out completely'. The University of Reading he thinks was 'hardly justifiable or necessary', as it could have been a college of Oxford or London; the robes have a 'very poor and defective system'. Sussex brings him forth at his most splenetic: the robes are 'the most deplorable, freakish, and unorthodox of any British University'. They are 'a calamity, because the writer could have given to Sussex the most

---

[12] Franklyn, *Academical Dress*, page 207.
[13] This was apparent at the start of his career, with the book *The Bearing of Coat-Armour by Ladies*: for a review of it and its errors, see page 107 below.
[14] Franklyn, *Academical Dress*, page 207. It is possible that he is objecting to the degree designations themselves – BDS, BEng, BTech, BMet – rather than to their content. But with Franklyn one never quite knows.

beautiful robes of all, reminiscent of the blue-green of the sea and the green of the Downs.'[15] He goes on to say that he is willing to design 'correct' robes for Sussex, and 'put her on a level with Oxford, Cambridge, Southampton and Hull'.

We pass then to his own creations for Southampton and Hull, and there is no lack of hubris. The Hull BD hood is 'the most handsome BD hood in the world',[16] while his suggestion for the Southampton MB would have made it 'one of the most beautiful and sought after MB hoods in the world'.[17] Based on his idea for the revised London MB, it was to be crimson silk, lined with peacock blue, and bound with crimson.[18] Mercifully, when the medical school was established in 1971, the university decided to give it a black shell, lined blue, and bound crimson, to keep it in line with other bachelors. It is not recorded what Franklyn thought of this, but we have seen that he was extremely angry with the Australian National University, another of his designs, when they had the temerity to design robes for their new bachelors' degrees and tinker with the scheme generally.

He passes over Wales, merely remarking that the faculties are listed in the wrong order – and misspelling Haycraft as Haycroft. His particular scorn is reserved for St David's College, Lampeter, but he reveals his total lack of any knowledge about the College.[19] It awarded a License [sic] in Divinity from 1884 to 1940: '... and one Diploma called "Lic.Div." How anyone could go about this world calling himself a 'Lic.Div.' is beyond the writer's imagination.' Indeed so: they did not.[20] The correct postnominal was LD: 'LicDiv' first appeared in the early editions of Haycraft, in which the unusual abbreviation LD was partially expanded to make it clear to readers what it stood for, and was copied unintelligently by every subsequent writer. He goes on: 'Whoever established this College must have been peculiar, to say the least, because no provision was made for their graduates to proceed to the MA and DD degrees, which every graduate should have the right to do'. Anyone at all familiar with the College's history (or indeed anyone claiming to be the sole expert on academic dress) knows that the right to award the BD was granted in 1852, thirty years after it was founded, and the BA in 1865, and they were hard-won privileges, but no provision was made for progression to the MA or the DD.[21] The BA hood, he thinks, is 'indescribably absurd'. As it is merely the Cambridge BA with a few black spots on the fur, it is hard

---

[15] Ibid., page 208. See above, page 74.

[16] Ibid., page 208.

[17] Ibid., page 209. Clearly even he could not out-design the Durham MB, which is the 'most beautiful MB hood in the world.' We merely note in passing the conceit that one would do a degree because of the hood it permits one to wear ...

[18] One has to wonder quite what he thought the crimson binding would have added, being as the shell was crimson to start with. But then he gave Laws the same blue as lines all the hoods, so the LL.B and LL.M hoods have the lining bound over.

[19] Franklyn, *Academical Dress*, page 209.

[20] Though several are now going about calling themselves LicDD. (This was a very short-lived post-PhD award, made by the College on its own authority, between 2007 and 2011.)

[21] Why provision was not made for progression to the MA at least, if not the DD, is unclear. This

to see why. It is arguably incorrect ('absurd' is too strong) insofar as other BA hoods are lined with rabbit-skin, while the Lampeter BA is described as lined with 'miniver' or 'ermine', even though it was always mock: rabbit-skin with black spots added. Miniver would, historically, make it an MA hood, as originally the difference lay in the quality of the fur. MAs adopted silk linings in the late Middle Ages, although the Oxford proctors retain the old miniver-lined MA hood.

The hood for the poor old 'LicDiv' is apparently 'not worth describing: in reality it is not a hood at all'. Full shape [f1], black stuff, lined black Italian cloth, bound 1" white silk: one wonders quite what feature stops it being a hood – and indeed what it is if it is not a hood. It was transferred to the DipTh in 1969, and died with that diploma in 1972.

Under Ireland, he gives modified praise to the New University of Ulster (as it then was; now simply the University of Ulster) as, although he drew up the principles (in a seven-page Memorandum)[22] and they were accepted, certain aspects were not quite as he desired – notably the shape of the hoods,[23] and the width of the binding on them. He describes the old Royal University of Ireland (RUI) as 'the Catholic university', which it was not:[24] the Roman Catholic Church saw it very much as a Protestant phenomenon, and forbade its members to attend it. It is true that the actual Catholic University became University College Dublin, part of the National University when that was set up in 1909, but that is not the same thing. More inaccuracy follows: '... but since the Irish Free State was established, it [the RUI] has changed to 'National', and all the hoods have become green!'. The NUI is thus dismissed, and no attempt is made to describe or analyse its (extremely logical and symmetrical) scheme of dress. The Irish Free State was, of course, not established until 1921.

Possibly his most egregious piece of refusal to accept correction comes in Chapter 13, where he deals with Lambeth degrees.[25] He had formed an idea that Lambeth degrees were awarded not by the Archbishop, but by the Crown – and thus outrank all other degrees.[26] Despite being told this was nonsense by both the then Archbishop (Cosmo Gordon Lang), and then by his Chaplain (Ian White-Thompson), by the Registrar of the Faculty Office (H T A Dashwood), and finally by a Lord Justice of the High Court of Appeal who was also a member of the Privy Council (he coyly says that he does not

---

was not rectified until 1971, when the charter was revised allowing the College to grant any degree, but it was immediately suspended, as the College became part of the University of Wales, and awarded its degrees.

[22] Franklyn, *Academical Dress*, page 209.

[23] Cambridge full [f1] with square capes.

[24] Franklyn, *Academical Dress*, page 210.

[25] A full critique of this is in: William Gibson, *Charles Franklyn's View on Lambeth Degrees*, in: *The History of Lambeth Degrees: Sources and Studies*, ed. by William Gibson, Burgon Society Historical Reprints 2, Burgon Society (2019) 129–138.

[26] This was founded on the fact that the degrees are confirmed by royal letters patent – which appears to be a late nineteenth-century innovation.

have permission to reveal his name), he refused to shift his position.

For one who was setting himself up to be the unimpeachable authority, ('as it is likely to be the standard work for some time')[27] the feet of clay appear all too often.

However, he does reveal sense at times. Under Leeds, he remarks that 'the system is not good, there is no clear or distinct Faculty colour, so that the system is a confused one. The academical dress of this university needs drastic revision'. This was true in 1970, and even more so now, as the University has title-specific hoods. As Leeds is one of those universities that seems to find it necessary to award a vast number of what Franklyn would regard as 'queer degrees and diplomas, that are not really proper degrees at all',[28] and gives each named degree its own hood, the system, based on three shades of green, is now in grave danger of falling apart.[29]

The best use of the book, therefore, is as a source-book for antiquarian articles, always with a very critical eye to his interpretations of what (he thinks) they say.

Degrees and Hoods of the World's Universities and Colleges, fifth edition

Franklyn was also, along with Frederick Rogers, George Shaw, and Hugh Boyd, asked to produce the fifth edition of Haycraft's *The Degrees and Hoods of the World's Universities and Colleges* in 1972. Each of the compilers initialled the entries he had submitted, but Franklyn

> took over the editorship – and possession of the whole project.
> He did not consult the other editors, but incorporated material
> as he saw fit.[30]

Certainly his initialled entries are far more prolix and opinionated than those of the other three – even more so those for universities which he had designed or revised the robes – and one can fairly easily pick up his 'revisions' to other entries. The Addendum is all his work, and contains another of his famous dismissive remarks. Of the Open University, he noted that requests had met with no response, and that possibly there was no academic dress in use.[31] 'A

---

[27] Letter, Franklyn to Francis Steer, 5 January 1971, tipped into the copy currently owned by Dr Paul Coxon.

[28] See above under Durham.

[29] In 2011, it was awarding sixteen bachelors' degrees, and twenty-two masters' degrees. Some, it is true, share hoods. See Nicholas Groves, ed., *Shaw's Academical Dress of Great Britain and Ireland*, vol. 1: *Degree-Awarding Bodies*, third edition, Burgon Society (2011), page 243ff. What would he have made of (for example) MPsObSt, MCFS, or BPerfArts?

[30] Alex Kerr and Mary Shaw, 'George Wenham Shaw, 1928–2006', *Transactions of the Burgon Society* 6 (2006) 8–11, page 10.

[31] This was probably the case in 1972. The OU (founded 1969, first students admitted 1971) had thought to do without academic dress, but (as with London in 1840) graduate pressure caused its introduction.

complete system could be designed in one hour' – which is a bit of a slap in the face for Southampton, Hull, etc, where he took many months in getting things sorted out.

Both these books were printed privately, by subscription; five hundred copies of *Degrees and Hoods*, and two hundred of *Academical Dress*. Each copy was numbered, and bears a manuscript note of who originally owned it, and to whom it was subsequently presented. All recipients were to 'write immediately to the author, acknowledge its safe arrival, and quote the number of the copy.' The author 'will be glad to buy back any copy that gets on to the market. This book should never be allowed out of the library to which it belongs.' So far as is known, no arrangements have been made since the author has ceased to be, and copies turn up on the open market – often sold off by the libraries which initially owned them.

Wills Cigarette Cards

One of the odder manifestations of public interest in academic dress was a series of cigarette cards produced by Wills in 1926, with commentary (and presumably the hoods chosen) by Franklyn. This I have dealt with in more detail in TBS 7,[32] but it is worth reiterating his extraordinary choice, given that he had only twenty-six cards: seven for Cambridge (BA, MA, MB, MD, MusB, ScD, and DD); five London (LL.D, MD, DLit, DSc, and BA); four Oxford (BA, MA, DLitt/DSc, and BCL/BM); Wales, Dublin, and Durham, two each (BA and MA); and one from the whole of Scotland – the Edinburgh MD. The text is, as I have noted, somewhat erratic, and bears the signs of a lack of careful (or possibly any) revision. The illustrations (which are of great use) were especially painted from life by AV Wheeler Holohan, who had designed a bookplate for Franklyn.

Monograph *Academic Costume*

A 'short monograph' on the topic was published in The Oxford Magazine of 6 and 13 February 1930, called 'Academic Costume'.[33] He deals with the subject under eight heads: Origin; The Hood; The Gown; Oxford and Cambridge Today; American Usage; Robes and Gowns; London University; Lambeth Degrees; and an appendix on The Chimere. Much of it was later reproduced in *Academical Dress*.

---

[32] Nicholas Groves, 'Popularizing University Hoods and Gowns: Will's Cigarette Cards, 1926', *Transactions of the Burgon Society* 7 (2007) 48–74.
[33] Here his post-nominals are MD, BS, MRCS(Eng), FSA(Scot).

Encyclopædia Britannica

Franklyn got his hands on the article on the Encyclopædia Britannica in 1941, and revised it for each fresh edition until his death.

Pears' Cyclopædia

The earlier editions simply listed the hoods in the form of a grid, universities along one axis, and degrees on the other. At some point (by 1964 at least) this was replaced by lists, and it would appear that Franklyn got his hands on this, too, as much of the descriptive wording is of his style: 'improved Burgon', etc, and Bristol has a note that 'This is an unconventional system', although the compiler may simply have been copying from a Franklyn source. He does not say that this is his work, however, and it may be that whoever edited this simply copied from him.

It is, therefore, difficult to avoid the conclusion that Franklyn's standing as the greatest expert on the subject of academic dress was founded to a great degree on his own self-promotion, and that his scholarship (if we can so designate something founded entirely on secondary sources and lack of rigorous research), as so often with such writers, had just enough accuracy as to make his other assertions appear to be true.

7 Heraldic and Genealogical Interests

Franklyn also knew a good deal about heraldry. Indeed, so highly did he regard his own abilities in this matter that he signed the 'Prologue' of his *Academical Dress* as 'Charles Franklyn, *creatione suâ* Blanch Lyon Herald Extra Ordinary'. While we may have our Walter Mitty secrets, it takes a certain kind of mind to be able to display them so blatantly in public – and in a work which is intended to be accepted as the ne plus ultra in a particular field of scholarship.[1] Needless to say, the College of Arms has never had such an official as Blanch Lyon Herald Extra Ordinary.[2] There is a White Lion Society, which is the 'society of friends' of the College of Arms, and it takes its name from the supporters of the College's coat-of-arms. It was not founded until 1984, but one wonders if the inspiration for Franklyn's 'title' was the same. Clearly it reflects the status he felt he should have held in respect of his knowledge – that of a herald of the College of Arms. In *Who's Who* for 1970 he states that he was 'Hon. Asst. to Editor Burke's Landed Gentry, Centenary (15th) edn, 1937, and to Editor Armorial Families, 7th edition, 1929–30 (2 vols):'[3] does the fact he was not asked again reveal that they found him difficult?

Heraldry

Franklyn's own arms

In the *Short Genealogical History* Franklyn is quite clear that 'of the ffranklyn or Franklyn families belonging to the 'noblesse', i.e., have legally borne Arms, there have been only four in the history of England', these being the families of Skipton-on-Craven, Yorks; of Chart Sutton, etc, Kent; of Moor Park, Herts,

---

[1] This self-creation was restated (along with much else) in his Will.

[2] The Extra Ordinary [*sic*] Heralds that have been created are: Arundel, Beaumont, Maltravers, New Zealand, Norfolk, Surrey, and Wales. There was at various times a real 'Blanche Lyon Pursuivant Extraordinary' at the College of Arms, so this may also be where Franklyn got his title from. Clearly he wasn't satisfied being merely a pursuivant, hence the self-promotion to herald. (I am grateful to Dr Nicholas Jackson for this information.)

[3] *Who's Who: an annual biographical dictionary*, London, A&C Black, 1970, *s.v.* Franklyn, Charles Aubrey Hamilton.

now extinct; and of Jamaica, his own branch. All the odder, then that Bernard Burke in his *General Armory* of 1884[4] lists twelve Franklin or Franklyn families with arms – of which the Jamaica branch is not one, as those arms, as we shall see, did not exist at that date. Franklyn also notes, as distinguished holders of the name, Benjamin Franklin the scientist and statesman, and Sir John Franklin, the Arctic explorer, but seems to think that neither of them bore arms, and that they were therefore not members of the 'noblesse'.[5] Burke records arms for both of them, with much of the same imagery.

The Kent Franklin family (in its various spellings) was granted arms under Letters Patent sometime between 1536 and 1549, as they were recorded by Sir Christopher Barker, who was Garter King of Arms between those dates.[6] They were granted to John Frankelyn of Chart Sutton, Kent, and in the *Genealogical History* (reproduced in a black-and-white drawing as the frontispiece) they are quartered with those of Scott of Smarden.

The Franklyn of Chart Sutton, etc, arms are:

> Gules, on a bend between two dolphins embowed or, three lions heads erased of the first; crest: a greyhound's head couped argent collared and between two wings gules.[7]

A silver tablespoon held in the National Maritime Museum, held as a relic of Sir John Franklin's last expedition of 1845–48, which was found in an abandoned boat at Erebus Bay, King William Island, in May 1859 by the McClintock Search Expedition of 1857–59, has the Franklin crest of the demi-conger eel between the branches on the handle, so that is most likely the source for Franklyn's crest, although John Franklin's has the eel's head erased.[8] Sir John's own arms, as given in a sketch by JR Scott, were:

> argent, on a bend engrailed gules between three griffons' heads erased 2 and 1, a fish naient between two martlets.[9] *Crest*: a fish haurient between two sprigs of laurel proper. *Motto*: NISU.

---

[4] Bernard Burke, *The General Armory of England, Scotland, Ireland, and Wales*, Harrison and Sons, London (1884).

[5] Franklyn, *SGH*, page 17.

[6] Information from a letter to Franklyn from Philip Cary, York Herald, dated 12 August 1931, reproduced on page 22 of *SGH* where they are quartered with the arms of Scott of Smarden. For a discussion of the book, see below.

[7] Burke, however, gives them as Argent, on a bend azure between two dolphins or, three lions' heads erased of the first; crest none given. As this would put the gold dolphins on a silver field, this must be an error. However, Burke notes 'another, tinctures reversed' which would give a blue field with a silver bend.

[8] National Maritime Museum, object ID AAA2484. McClintock described finding eight pieces of plate in the boat with Franklin's crest. See https://collections.rmg.co.uk/collections/objects/2482.html (accessed 14 August 2020)

[9] MS drawing of the arms held in the National Library of Australia, in the scrapbook of James Reid Scott. Bib ID: 607523. Available online at https://catalogue.nla.gov.au/Record/607523 (accessed 15 August 2020) They are impaled with the arms of his wife, Jane Griffin: sable, a griffon segreant. Is it possible that the fish given for the crest is in fact mistaken for a badly-drawn demi-conger eel?

Scott noted that these were drawn from an engraving on a goblet, so it was 'hatched', and he noted that the tincture of the griffons' heads was not given. He thought that the fishes and the martlet were 'probably' argent.[10]

However, although on his second bookplate Franklyn describes himself as 'of Kidbrooke, Com Kent':[11] he was nothing of the kind, as he himself says the descent cannot be proved. He tells us in *SGH* that his branch of the family is traceable back to a 'John Franklyn (or Frankling)' recorded in 1678 as living in the North Sound Division of the island of Antigua, but

> whence came this man we do not know. He may have come out direct from England in 1654, or he may have immigrated with some of the early settlers from the mainland of America in the 1630–50 period.[12]

Figure 26: The arms of Charles Franklyn

The form of the arms used by Franklyn himself is, therefore, neither of these (see Figure 26). They are reproduced as a seal on page 59 of *SGH*.[13] These are blazoned:

> Sable, on a bend invected between two martlets or, a dolphin hauriant proper between a lion's head and a leopards' head

---

[10] Burke, *General Armory* gives them as Argent, on a bend azure 3 dolphins of the field. But they are very similar to the coat he gives for 'Co York', reading lions' heads for gryphons.

[11] The ancestral village of the Kent Franklins.

[12] Franklyn, *SGH*, page 61. There is a footnote speculating on his origin, either a son of William Franklyn of St Clement Danes, or 'sprung from' John Franklyn of Kent.

[13] The Contents page refers to a 'colour plate' – possibly the same as the one in *The Bearing of Coat-Armour by Ladies* – but it is not reproduced in the digitized copy.

both erased gules. *Crest*: a demi-conger-eel erect or, between two sprigs of hawthorn fructed proper.[14]

These were

> granted by Letters Patent under the hand and seal of Sir Henry Farnham Burke, KCVO, CB, FSA, Garter King of Arms, to all the descendants of Henry Franklin, Esq, MLA, Jamaica, and are duly recorded with pedigree in HM College of Arms.

Burke granted the arms in 1923.[15] This is a 'retrospective and confirmatory grant',[16] with a shield contrived to echo, but not reproduce, the other Franklin arms, a standard heraldic practice where direct descent cannot be proven. We may, therefore, assume that Franklyn designed these arms himself, using elements from the other Franklin arms. They are shown in *The Bearing of Coat Armour by Ladies*, for some reason anonymously.[17] Given the date (1923), does this possibly mean that he had designed the arms, but not had them confirmed – and thus explains the 'confirmatory' part of the grant? Or were they in fact being used by Henry, but irregularly ('assumed')?

This retrospective grant has the odd result that (assuming Franklyn did design the arms) not only Henry, but a large number of his descendants, went to their graves not knowing that they would be (were?) entitled to arms!

It would be interesting to know why Franklyn chose Henry as the grantee: going back three generations is highly unusual – and more expensive! One generation is the usual, and occasionally two.[18] Possibly as it was his widow who brought their children to England and gave rise to the English branches of the family of which he was part. Henry Franklin (1811–57) died in Kingston, and his widow came to England with the children in 1859.[19] He was a lawyer, and deputy Judge Advocate, as well as sitting as a Member of the Legislative Assembly.[20]

So far as the continuance of the arms is concerned, Henry had nine children, of whom five were sons. Two of them died in infancy; of the other three one had a daughter only, who never married. So they descend via Franklyn's grandfather to him and his brother, and via his great-uncle James, through his sons George (married, but no children) and Henry, who had a son, Charles

---

[14] Franklyn, *SGH*, page 58.

[15] Will, Clause XIII (e).

[16] William Shakespear did exactly the same, having the arms granted to his father, so they descended through his brother also. Franklyn also (see below) expresses extreme irritation that no-one in his mother's family had seen fit to do likewise.

[17] Plate III: 'The armorial bearings of a gentleman'; Plate VII: 'The arms of a maiden lady, the daughter of the gentleman whose achievement is shown in Plate III'.

[18] The heralds charge per generation included! (Personal communication, Dr John Horton).

[19] Franklyn, *SGH*, page 71. It is not known why she did so.

[20] The House of Assembly was the Jamaican legislature which operated 1664 to 1865, when it voted that Jamaica became a crown colony. It was dominated by the white planter class, as the property qualification was very high; while the qualification to be an elector was not so high, it still effectively excluded non-whites.

Peter Damien, and a daughter. It is not known if he had any children. If not, then the arms died out in that branch, and of course they died with Franklyn on his branch. This clearly explains the extraordinary rigmarole he sets out in the codicil to the will, leaving £5000 so that his sister's granddaughter could, on her marriage, get a royal licence to bear the Franklyn arms quartered with those of her paternal grandfather (Owen) – and requiring her husband to obtain a grant if he was not already armigerous.

However, in his will, Franklyn makes the following extraordinary statement:[21]

> A serious mistake was made in the blazon of my Arms in the retrospective and confirmatory Patent issued by the late Sir Henry Farnham Burke in 1923, and there was also an error in depicting the Arms in the margin of the Patent. The 'bend' was drawn 'invected' when it should have been 'engrailed' and the lower lion's head erased was called a leopard's head and was painted as a dotted thing like a red and black Dalmatian dog's. Apart from the Dolphin on the bend at the fesse point both the upper and the lower charges on the bend should be 'lion's heads erased gules'. All lions or lions' heads drawn in profile are lions or lions' heads respectively, a leopard being the correct term when 'guardant', i.e., when looking out of the shield. (In the Royal Arms of England the three animals are leopards, i.e., three lions passant guardant and the word 'leopard' implies a lion that is passant and is looking at one.) My trustees are asked to note that the correct blazon of our family Arms should be: Sable, on a bend engrailed between two martlets or, a dolphin haurient proper between two lions heads erased gules.

He is quite wrong about the leopard's head:

> Arthur Charles Fox-Davies wrote in 1909 that the distinction between lions (which were constantly rampant) and leopards (which were necessarily walking) originated in French heraldry and was brought into English heraldry along with so much else of English language and custom deriving from French traditions. But 'the use of the term leopard in heraldry to signify a certain position for the lion never received any extensive sanction, and has long since become obsolete in British armory,' though the distinction is still observed in French blazon.[22]

---

[21] Clause XIII (e). Punctuation added. We are treated to another mini-lecture. The rest of Clause XIII is concerned with his house.

[22] https://en.wikipedia.org/wiki/Leopard_(heraldry), referencing A C Fox-Davies, *A Complete Guide to Heraldry*, T C and E C Jack, London (1909), page 173. I am grateful to Dr John Horton for this reference.

Where did it come from, if it is not another lion's head? With the exception of two very different coats, those given by Burke all involve a bend, a dolphin, two or more lions' heads, and martlets.

This raises a number of questions. First, why did he not have the initial patent corrected before it was issued? Did he not check it as it was being prepared? Second, why did he use the 'incorrect' form throughout his life (as on his bookplates) and not what he says is the 'correct' form, and only raise the matter in the will? And what are the descendants supposed to do about it? The 'incorrect' form are the arms shown on colour plates III and VII in *The Bearing of Coat Armour by Ladies*, and also quite specifically as 'the armorial bearings of the family of Franklin or Franklyn, of Kingston, Jamaica' on page 59 of *SGH*.

However, as we have seen, with Franklyn 'should' often means 'it would, in my opinion, be a good idea if ...': as, for example, with the bachelors' hoods at Birmingham and Exeter, where he says they 'should' be lined with white in addition to the faculty border, which could imply, on one reading, that in fact they were, and that it had come to be omitted. So, do 'should' and 'mistake' here refer to what he wanted and was told he could not have? The confusion over the lion's and leopard's head is a minor heraldic quibble; the bend is intriguing: all the coats recorded in Burke have the bend with plain edges, but there is one, for a family in Yorkshire, in which it is engrailed. The substitution of invected for engrailed (or *vice versa*) is a common way of differencing coats for different branches of a family.

Bookplates

Franklyn had a number of heraldic bookplates, two of which appear in *SGH* and also on the website *The Cyber Journal of Heraldic Bookplates*.[23] Both show the so-called 'incorrect' arms.

The first bookplate (see Figure 27), designed by Ambrose Vincent Wheeler Holohan,[24] is dated 1923:

'Charles Aubrey Hamilton Franklyn, of The Corner House, Lincoln, Esqre, MD' – which has the unfortunate effect of implying that either the house or the city is an Esquire and a Doctor of Medicine. It is differenced with a crescent, the sign of a second son, which he was not, although his father was. The poor old 'Dalmatian dog' can be seen as the lowest of the charges on the bend.

The second (see Figure 28) is rather more pretentious ('An unique heraldic design'). It was 'drawn to the author's instructions by the late John R Suther-

---

[23] http://www.bookplate.info/Bookplate/britain_7.htm (accessed 24 August 2020). It appears to have been abandoned, the last updates being in 2006.
[24] Holohan (1889–1938) also painted the illustrations of the hoods for the Wills' cigarette card series. In *SGH* he is given as 'Major V Wheeler-Holohan (a King's Messenger)'.

Figure 27: Franklyn's bookplate (first version)

land, Hon Heraldic Artist to The Court of The Lord Lyon King of Arms'.[25] (Sutherland died in 1933). The version in *SGH* has the dexter banner with the Franklyn arms on; a later version, with the Exeter College arms, must be a later refinement after his time at Oxford. The shield is held by an eagle, which also grasps two banners. The difference between the two heads on the bend is less marked – and the dots have vanished.

The inscription is in mediæval French:

Carolus le Frankeleyn de Kidbrooke, com Kent, armiger, MD.

'de Kidbrooke' is a piece of licence: one of the original Franklin families came from that village.

The motto has changed from Pro Rege, Patria et Familia (for King, Country, and Family) to Hold Fast. This he notes as 'my slogan or personal motto',[26] and he requests that it 'shall be incorporated into the full armorial achievement and shall be borne by my heirs and successors'. The differencing crescent has vanished, also. The inclusion of the Exeter College banner is, as we have seen, definitely exaggerating his connexion with the college. The coronet is very similar to the one he later designed for the Transport Commission – here it has two roses between three oak-leaves, and is presumably meant to denote 'Englishness' – which, given his political views, is unsurprising; it is not one of those recognized by the College of Arms; this may also explain 'Hold Fast'. Note also the oak leaves and rose by the eagle's feet. This display can be best explained by the extraordinary stipulations in

---

[25] Franklyn, *SGH*, page 93.
[26] Will, Clause XIII, (e), page 9.

Figure 28: Franklyn's bookplate (second version)

his Will (see Chapter 8).

Heraldic designs by Franklyn

In addition to the strong likelihood that he designed his own arms, Franklyn is known to have designed the arms of St Peter's Hall (now College), Oxford, in 1929, and of the borough of Bridgnorth in 1958; and also the first badge of the British Transport Commission, which was painted on all British trains, in 1956. In *Who's Who* for 1970 he states that he had designed 'armorial ensigns and 3 badges, British Transport Commn 1956; Arms of Borough of Bridgenorth, 1959', but he omits the arms of St Peter's College.

St Peter's College, Oxford

The College was founded in 1929, as St Peter's Hall, by Francis James Chavasse, Bishop of Liverpool, who was concerned at the rising cost of education in the older universities in Britain, and projected St Peter's as a college where promising students, who might otherwise be deterred by the costs of college life elsewhere, could obtain an Oxford education. It became a full College of Oxford University in 1961.

In the same year the Hall was granted its coat of arms (see Figure 29), which incorporates the arms of Bishop Chavasse on the sinister side, and a device representing the church of St Peter-le-Bailey (now the College chapel, and from which the College takes its name) on the dexter: a green field, with the crossed keys of St Peter surmounted by a representation of Oxford Castle. The two are united into one coat by a gold border.

Figure 29: Arms of St Peter's College, Oxford

As Franklyn had written a genealogy of the Chavasse family in 1929, this may well explain how the connexion came about – though it may equally well be the other way round! How he got into contact with Chavasse is not known.

British Transport Commission

This emblem[27] was a familiar sight on the sides of railway carriages until BR invented its double arrow 'Coming and Going' logo. It is taken from the crest of the full achievment of the BTC (registered at the College of Arms and by the Lord Lyon in 1956), which was designed 'in consultation with armorial expert CAH Franklyn' (see Figure 30).[28] The desire for a coat-of-arms was that of the new Chairman of the Commission, Sir Brian Robertson: apparently he had seen the armorial achievement of the (former) Great Eastern Railway in a BR office, and decided that the Commission should have proper arms also. There was at that time a desire to return to traditional-style liveries and emblems.[29] It is not clear how Franklyn came by the commission – it is very unlikely that he knew Robertson personally[30] – though very possibly he simply wrote and put himself forward as he did with the universities.

It was not universally popular: Tanya Jackson says that traditionalists found it 'a very pleasing design', while those with a more progressive outlook

---

[27] Known by BR employees as the 'ferret and dartboard' – not something one imagines Franklyn would have appreciated!

[28] Tanya Jackson, *British Rail: The Nation's Railway*, The History Press, Stroud (2013), page 95. She has a good discussion of its reception and use – and also its various versions. As noted above, in *Who's Who* he stated that he designed it.

[29] Personal communication, Dr David Lawrence, Kingston University; e-mail dated 22 August 2020.

[30] General Sir Brian Robertson, Bt, Chairman 1953–61. He spent both wars fighting abroad, and the interim period (1934–40) as managing director of Dunlop Rubber in South Africa. Later Baron Robertson of Oakridge.

Figure 30: The arms of the British Transport Commission

thought it was an 'heraldic abortion'.[31] She thought it resembled 'a lion holding a wheel whilst springing out of a mess of ribbons [the mantling] – like a bimbo out of a birthday cake'.[32] She goes on to say that 'beneath it is a shield with three wheels, some blue wavy lines and a portcullis being propped up by what look like two *Star Trek* aliens, both with wheels pinned to their chests'. Franklyn has met his match.

The blazon is:

> Vert, on a fess argent, two barrulets wavy azure doubly cotised, between in chief three railway-wheels and in base a portcullis of the second, chained or.
> *Crest*: on a wreath of the colours a demi-lion rampant gules, langued and armed azure, holding a railway-wheel argent.
> *Supporters*: two lions rampant guardant gules, langued azure, charged on the chest with a railway-wheel argent.

The symbolism is as follows: the silver fess on green represents the roads crossing the countryside, while the double cotising represents the railways. The barrulets presumably indicate water-transport. The wheels of course represent the locomotives and rolling-stock, while the portcullis symbolizes the ports. The lions are, presumably, taken from the royal heraldry of England and Scotland. Thus the coat incorporates British Railways, roads and road transport, canals and waterways, and ports and harbours.

The full achievement was not used on trains, but an emblem based on the

---

[31] *Modern Railways*, January 1965, page 3, quoted in Jackson, *British Rail*, page 95. This is much stronger language than CAHF ever employed about things he disapproved of! But it is interesting to see him receiving this treatment.
[32] Ibid., page 95.

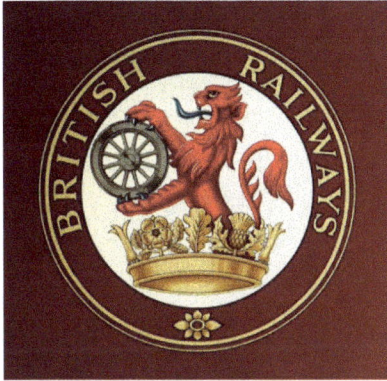

Figure 31: The 'Ferret and Dartboard' emblem of the British Transport Commission

crest (see Figure 31).[33] From a coronet composed of the national flowers of the various countries of the United Kingdom (but note England is represented twice, with a rose and an oak-leaf, and Wales gets two leeks, while Scotland gets only a single thistle), a lion rises, holding a wheel. In the arms, the demi-lion issues directly from a wreath, so the coronet is probably Franklyn's invention: it is not dissimilar to the one on his second bookplate (*vide supra*). Even this was not popular: the in-house *British Railways Magazine* for August put this new visual identifier on page 3, with the cover being reserved for 'a picture of ticket clerks busily giving advice on holiday journeys'.[34] It came in two principal forms: one with British Railways written around it in circular border, and one with the words in 'wings' either side.

Bridgnorth Borough Council[35]

The arms, granted on 14 September 1958 to Bridgnorth Borough Council are:

> Argent on a Rock in base a Castle of three Towers with spires proper from the dexter spire a Banner of St. George and from the sinister spire a Banner quarterly Gules a Lion passant Or and Azure a Fleur de Lys also Or on a Chief Vert a Lion passant guardant Gold. The motto, Fidelitas Urbis Salus Regis (The faithfulness of the city is the safety of the King). (See Figure 32.)

The arms are based upon the former seal, dating from the fifteenth century, which was displayed on a shield before the current arms were granted. The seal bore a castle with a central tower, and on either side a shield, bearing the arms now on the banners. The castle represents that built in 1098 by Robert de Belesme, Earl of Shrewsbury, who held it in rebellion against Henry I.

---

[33] It was used as the helmet-plate by British Transport Police.
[34] Jackson, *British Rail*, page 96.
[35] This became Bridgnorth Town Council in 1974.

Figure 32: The arms of Bridgnorth Borough Council

During the Civil War the castle was besieged by the Parliamentary forces and finally demolished. The motto refers to the town's support of the Royalist cause, and was created by the Revd George Bellett, Vicar 1835–70.

There is an account of this in *The Birmingham Post* for 10 April, 1959. The town had been using the triple-towered castle emblem since at least 1623, when it was recorded in an heraldic visitation of that date that the town had no arms. Franklyn is quoted as saying that 'the device was heraldically unsound'. The newspaper account says that it had been

> amended by an expert, Dr Charles Franklyn. He has added a Royal lion – 'the finest in all heraldry', he said at the ceremony – in the top third of the arms, recalling Bridgnorth's ancient connection with the Crown. Other slight amendments have made the device heraldically perfect, and Dr Franklyn was able to assure the Mayor: 'You have a banner not surpassed by any town or city in England'.[36]

Again, how he came by the commission is not known.

The Bearing of Coat-Armour by Ladies

Franklyn published this book in 1923 – at which date he was still Franklin.[37] It must be granted that it is more coherently written than the later *Academical Dress*, but one might be forgiven for wondering why the first forty pages (of 132) are taken up with explaining the basics of heraldry: something one would assume that a reader would already know. Not only that, but the final forty pages are given over to considering 'the uses and applications of heraldry', and 'heraldry as an art – or the consideration of the artistic side

---

[36]The Birmingham Post, 10 April, 1959, page 7.

[37]Charles A H Franklin, *The Bearing of Coat-Armour by Ladies, A Guide to the Bearing of Arms by Ladies of All Ranks, Whether Maid, Wife, or Widow, in England, Scotland, & Ireland*, John Murray, London (1923). Reprinted by the Genealogical Publishing Co, of Baltimore, MD, in 1973. (I am grateful to Dr Alex Kerr for this information.) He lists himself on the title page as MRCS(Eng), FSA(Scot), LRCP(Lond) – so no mention of the bogus MA and BSc.

of an achievement'. It starts with a pedantic disquisition on the difference between 'heraldry' and 'armory' as terms. Plate III, captioned 'The Armorial Bearings of a Gentleman' are those of Franklyn himself, which he does not say: possibly we are assumed to know this. There is no bibliography, and only a very few discursive footnotes, so it is not possible to say what his sources were, beyond vague attributions in the text.[38] These are, of course, all faults which were to be reproduced fifty years later in *Academical Dress*.

To a degree, the entire basis of the book may be mistaken. His statement 'When heraldry was in the making, no allowances were made for the bearing of arms by women'[39] was challenged by Thomas Innes of Learney in his Scots Heraldry, who says:

> The idea that heraldry did not cater for women is a fallacy which has grown out of the equally unfounded idea that heraldry was concerned with war, and not – as it really is – much more with civil and domestic life.'[40]

The book received a blistering review in the Antiquaries' Journal in April 1924 by L F Salzman.[41] It is worth quoting in full.

> It is remarkable that heraldry should be regarded as a subject on which any one who is capable of reading is also capable of writing. No research or knowledge of original sources is considered necessary; it is sufficient to make a re-hash of the statements found in modern text-books, without attempting to verify them. The one original contribution to this book appears to be the statement (on p 79) that 'John, Earl of Eltham [*sic*], second son of Edward II, bore England without [*sic*] a bordure of France, denoting his descent from a French mother'. Mr Franklin is a devout worshipper at the shrine of the College of Arms and a profound admirer of the Prophet of Heralds, Mr Fox-Davies. We are therefore treated to the statement that, 'Any man who is lawfully entitled to bear arms is not, and

---

[38] We also get a couple more insights into his opinions. On page x, we are told (though remembering he wrote in 1923) that '... women have recently begun to invade all the professions and actually to sit in the House of Commons. And if they go still further, and succeed in being summoned to the House of Lords in respect to peerages which they hold in their own right ...'. And yet: he notes on page 59, that in the Middle Ages, women occasionally sat in the Lords in their own right – but then, on page 93, that their husbands sat for them.

[39] Franklin, *The Bearing of Coat-Armour by Ladies*, page 93.

[40] Thomas Innes of Learney, *Scots Heraldry*, Oliver and Boyd (1938), pages 157–158 (second edition 1956). Innes was Lord Lyon King of Arms 1945–69. His remark is true: only a very little thought will show how useless painted shields and embroidered surcoats are in the filth and turmoil of a mediæval battle-field.

[41] L F Salzman, "The Bearing of Coat-Armour by Ladies' by Charles A H Franklin', *The Antiquaries Journal* 4 (2 Apr. 1924) 171–172. Published online by Cambridge University Press, 8 January 2012. Louis Francis Salzman, CBE, MA(Cantab), Hon DLitt(Sussex) (1878–1971) was an economic historian who specialized in the mediæval period, though he had originally intended to work in medicine. He was the General Editor of the Victoria County History from 1934 to 1949. He lived in Lewes from 1934, so must have been known to Franklin.

cannot be, a commoner, but is a nobleman', and are given a full price-list of the College of Arms and of the cheaper rival establishment presided over by Ulster King of Arms.

By an unconscious stroke of humour Mr Franklin demolishes at one blow the shrine before which he would have us join him in worship. On p 73 he portrays the armorial bearings of 'Geraldine Susan Maud, daughter of JEG de Montmorency, Esq, MA(Cantab), Barrister-at-Law, Quain Professor of Law, University of London, a Cadet of the noble House of de Montmorency (Viscount), (Arms recorded in Ulster Office; pedigree in Ulster Office and College of Arms)'. The arms, which are as 'genuine' as the payment of fees can make them, are based on those of the great de Montmorency, whose name the Irish family of Morres assumed in 1815 on the strength of a pedigree which has received the official blessing, but of which Dr Round does not hesitate to say, and to prove conclusively, (*Feudal England*, 519–27) that 'a more impudent claim was never successfully foisted on the authorities and public'.

The book is not redeemed by its illustrations, as the author is almost entirely lacking in artistic discernment: almost – not quite, for although he assures us that 'Any one who is really entitled to arms should avoid paintings done outside HM Offices of Arms', he very rightly denounces the design issued by the College of Arms for the 'married achievement of Princess Mary and Lord Lascelles', and rejects the 'utterly grotesque' official design for the arms of the Duke and Duchess of York. It is perhaps as a subtle proof of the danger of employing unofficial draughtsmen that he reproduces a feeble drawing of the arms of Lord Lascelles, in colours, with the intriguing motto, *In solo Deus salus*.

This may well explain why he never attempted another work on heraldry. We might be charitable and remark that, as it was published in 1923, he was a full-time medical student while writing it.

Genealogy

Franklyn's genealogical publications take the form of eight 'genealogical histories' of various families, all printed in extremely small runs, obviously for internal family consumption. I am unsure how he came by the commissions to write them. Of these, two are 'supplements to' other works, one was written in collaboration, and one (*The Genealogy of Anne the Quene*) was published in a magazine.

Of these, the *Short Genealogical & Heraldic History of the Families of Frankelyn of Kent and Franklyn of Antigua & Jamaica, B.W.I.* may stand as an example.[42] Although it was published by a commercial firm, it was limited to seventy copies. One of these, number twenty-eight, has been digitized by Internet Archive,[43] and number fourteen is in the possession of Arthur Casey.

All copies have a page reading

> Privately printed, limited to 70 copies, of which this is
> No ....
> (Signed) [CAH Franklyn]

with the number filled in by hand, and signed by Franklyn; no 28 has a further MS note 'corrected CAHF 2/3/37', and the corrections are indeed made to the printed text in his hand. There is a list of subscribers, among whom are several Franklins (with divers spellings of the name!), located in the USA and Australia, as well as the UK.[44] It also includes two members of the Bolton family, which, given that his marriage to Erica Bolton had been annulled that year, is interesting.[45] He also deposited copies in the British Museum Library, the Bodleian Library, Oxford, and the University Library, Cambridge.

The Contents page states that the work is divided into five sections:

I. Introduction: The Frankeleyn or Franklyn in Mediæval Times and the principal Francklyn, Franklyn of [*sic*; misprint for 'or'] ffranklyn Families

II. The Family of Frankelyn, Francklyn or Franklyn of Kent

III. The Family of Fanklyn or Franklin of Antigua and Jamaica, with de Trafford of Trafford connection, and the Armorial Bearings and Bookplates of various members of the Family.

IV. The Family of Bolton of Sandford, Enstone and Wootton, and Witney, Co Oxon, and that of Dickeson of Rochester, Co Kent.

V. The Family of Gray of Billericay and Chelmsford, Co Essex.

Section IV is indeed a sad reminder of the (non-)marriage. Clearly this work was planned before things came to grief: indeed, he notes on page 114 that the genealogy was 'worked out by the author of this book in 1929'. It is interesting that he left it in, as the sole connexion of the two families was by

---

[42] Charles A H Franklyn, *A Short Genealogical & Heraldic History of the Families of Frankelyn of Kent and Franklyn of Antigua & Jamaica, B.W.I.*, E O Beck (1930). Already referred to as SGH.

[43] https://archive.org/details/shortgenealogica00fran/mode/2up (accessed 14 August 2020). It belongs to the Allen County Public Library Genealogy Center in Fort Wayne, Indiana.

[44] All the US subscribers were in New York, so it would be interesting to learn how the copy ended up in Indiana.

[45] One was her brother, Ronald.

the marriage, and it is not referred to in the text. His former wife is listed on page 110 as 'issue' of Felix Dickeson Bolton, and noted as:

> Erica Milly, b 24th Oct, 1905, at Dover, bapt. at the Church of the Annunciation, Chislehurst, Kent; *unmarried* 1937. [my emphasis][46]

Franklyn justifies the inclusion, however, on page 102, by saying that

> This section on the Bolton family is included within this work mainly in order to preserve from destruction what at present exists only in the Records of the College of Arms, and in two MSS. certified copies of this very remarkable pedigree, held by FD and LH Bolton, respectively, under the signature of the present Garter King of Arms. It was an old family Diary that finally led to this long and truly remarkable lineage being unfolded.[47]

All the odder, then, that it precedes the section on the Grays, from whom he descended via his mother.

Of the Gray family, he notes that:

> This family has no Armorial bearings at present (neither Arms nor Crest) inasmuch as no member of the family has up to the present time, either proved a right to Arms by proving and registering in the College of Arms in London, a direct male descent from some Gray to whom Arms were granted or confirmed and registered in the past, or obtained a Grant of Arms for the Gray family by Letters Patent ... A Grant of Arms by Patent should have been obtained about 1800 by Andrew and Sarah Gray, which would then have covered in scope all the Grays living today and all their descendants in all time coming. A retrospective grant could have been obtained by the late Charles Harrison Gray or Walter Gray during their lives for all the descendants of their grandfather, the aforesaid Andrew Gray. The opportunity has been missed, at the best, it would mean now a series of separate Grants to the heads of the several branches in order to cover all Andrew's descendants to this day: evidently the Essex air is not particularly invigorating![48]

One can sense the frustration that his mother's family is not armigerous, and his irritation that they had not bothered with getting arms, and especially with Andrew Gray: not that it would have done Franklyn any good if they had, as she would not have been an heraldic heiress, and so he could not have

---

[46] One would like to know quite how much irritation he was caused by her continuing to call herself Mrs Franklin.

[47] The cynic might wonder if Franklyn married not Erica Bolton, but her lineage. She was entitled to bear her father's arms of Bolton quartered with Dickeson.

[48] Franklyn, *SGH*, page 139. It is followed by a long discussion on why certain existing Gray arms are not applicable.

quartered her arms with his. (And recall that, when rejected as the designer of the academic dress at Essex, he suddenly needed to boast of his 300-year descent in the county!) It is also hard to see why a later descendant could not have got a grant for Andrew: after all, Franklyn got his retrospective grant for his great-grandfather.

The book is exceptionally difficult to use, as he includes no pedigrees ('family trees') beyond a few for the section on the Gray family and its connexions. Following the style of Burke's Landed Gentry,[49] it is set out in prose, with no family trees, but with useful information on each person. Following the lines of descent is therefore tiresome, as he deals with the children of the eldest son, then those of the second son ('of whom we treat later', which may be anything from two lines to several pages later: there are few internal references), etc, then the daughters, regardless of their actual ages, and there is no clear means of cross-referencing: one needs to recall exactly which form of numbering (I, (1), 1., a), i ...) refers to which generation, where he decides to start numbering afresh – and the numbering system can change at random. There is also no name index.[50] For example, going back to his great-grandfather Henry:

Henry Franklin (1840–99) had issue:

(1) James (1838–94)
    1. George Frederick Edward Essex (1863–)
    2. Henry Walter (1867–1915)
        a) Charles Peter Damian (1890–)
           i) David Cyril (1929–)
           ii) Ann Rowland (1931–)
        b) Katherine Violet Cecilia Mary (1897–)
    3. Violet Alice Maud (1866–1925)
        a) Humphrey Edmund (1891–)
        i–iv [children]
        b) Rudolph
        i [child]
(2) Henry (1867–1915)
(3) Charles (1842–87)
    1. Herbert Charles Temple (1865–1916)
    2. Aubrey Hamilton (1868–1921)
        a) Charles Aubrey Hamilton (1896–)
        b) Harold Gordon (1904–)
        c) Irene Hamilton (1900–)

---

[49] A book which seems to have occupied the same place in his affections as the *Baronetage* did in those of Sir Walter Elliott of Kellynch in *Persuasion* – Franklyn even borrowed the form of its full title, *A Genealogical and Heraldic History of the Landed Gentry of Great Britain and Ireland*. Franklyn was involved in the centenary edition of 1937 as 'Editor's Honorary Assistant, and mentioned and thanked in the Preface' (will, Clause IX, iii). This was 'the best ever edition' (ibid.).

[50] The great boon of its being available online is that it is searchable.

(4) Alice Elizabeth (1846–1893)

(5) Emily (1851–1913)

(6) Julia (1853–)

Each of these has a paragraph or more attached with details of birth, education, marriage, employment, distant connexions with people he regarded as important, etc. So, while there is an internal logic to this, the discursive material defeats it. As an example, we may take that for Julia:

> Julia, b 26th Feb. 1853, bapt. 4th July 1853 at Kingston, mar, 1st July 1875, William Hunter Hutchinson (son of John Hutchinson, MRCS(Eng) of Donington, Co Lincoln, by Isabella his wife (b. 2nd Aug. 1817, bapt at St Margaret's, Westminster, 27th May 1818) dau. of George Ebenezer Williams, DMus, [footnote: Who d. 17 April 1819 æt 35, buried in the S. Cloister of the Abbey] organist of Westminster Abbey), and d 3rd Dec. 1907, leaving issue by him who d. 10th July 1931 at [address] and was cremated at Golders Green Cemetery, two sons (of whom the younger, Rev Charles William Hutchison, is unmar. 1937), and two daus., Isabel, unmar, and Muriel, d 1931.[51]

This needs careful reading to avoid assuming that the father of her children was the late Organist of the Abbey – it was her husband's maternal grandfather! And is not quite clear if it was she or her husband who was cremated.

As already noted, the other genealogical works are extremely difficult to source, but it is assumed that they follow much the same format.

---

[51]Franklyn, *SGH*, page 82. Williams was Organist of the Abbey 1814–19.

8 He, being dead, yet speaketh...[1]

As has become apparent throughout this work, Franklyn had an extremely controlling nature. This is clearly expressed in his Will, along with some other even less desirable traits. The document is twelve pages long, plus a five-page Codicil.

It starts by stating that it is the last Will and Testament 'of me Charles Aubrey Hamilton Franklyn', followed by thirteen lines giving his various statuses. It is worth quoting in full, as it gives an excellent picture of how he thought of himself:[2]

> Doctor in Medicine, Bachelor in Surgery, Master of Arts and Doctor of Letters 'honoris causâ',[3] a Member of the Royal College of Surgeons of England, a Licentiate of the Royal College of Physicians of London, a Fellow of the Linnean Society of London, a Fellow of the Society of Antiquaries of Scotland, sometime a Fellow of the Royal Society of Medicine; Bedell of Convocation in the University of London 'sine die' from 1932, Member of the Standing Committee 1927–61 (Senior Member 1954–61), a Provincial Supervisor in charge of Final Degree Examinations (June) 1941–56; Physician; Consultant in Academical Dress; Herald Genealogist (Blanch Lyon Herald Extra Ordinary creatione suâ); Designer of the Complete System of Academical and Official Robes for five British Universities; who served in the Great War 25th November 1915 to 9th February 1919 as Lieutenant RA(SR), holder of the King's Medal for the Great War 1914–18 and of the Allies' Victory Medal; and but for the disbandment of the Special Reserve in April 1920 to save paying our retaining fee of Twenty pounds per annum 'de jure' Lieutenant-Colonel RA(SR) and a Colonel in the Army.

---

[1]Hebrews 11:4
[2]Will, page 1. I have silently added punctuation throughout to the original for the sake of legibility.
[3]This is interesting, as he usually insisted degrees are *in* a particular faculty – as he has listed the MD and BS. Note also the omission of the 'degrees' from Lincoln-Jefferson and Intercollegiate – and also the FPhS.

Clause I appoints his executors and trustees. Clause II makes interesting reading. It says that, although he has remained in close and friendly touch with his younger brother, he is making no provision for him, 'as for many years he enjoyed a salary more than twice my income and had the same small private income as myself' he received more than £700 from aunts 'that I did not', and since his retirement has enjoyed a pension 'twice the size of my income'; he has no issue, and 'he has the opportunity to save and invest a large amount between 1922 and 1953. It is the young ones we must think about.' But his brother predeceased him in any case, earlier in 1982.

Clause III deals with his beloved cat, Peerless Red Rupert. He was a pedigree animal, a short-hair red tabby, and we are told this, along with his parents' names and his registration number with the Cat Fancy. He was 'to my mind the most beautiful and dignified creature on this planet'.[4] He was to be taken care of by his niece, who was to receive £5.00 a quarter for his upkeep.

> He should be brushed every morning about 9.45. a.m. and be combed thoroughly every night with Spratt's No. 6 chromium-plated cat comb at 9.30 p.m. before being given his last saucer of milk and being put to bed at 9.40 p.m.

This is followed by detailed instructions as to what is to happen when the cat dies – the dimensions of the wooden box, the nature of wrapping (linen, double thickness), place of burial, the fact that there is to be a stone, and the grave maintained.[5]

Clause IV details his directions for his own burial. The funeral was to take place at All Saints, Putney, with interment at Putney Vale Cemetery in his grandfather's grave (Charles Franklyn, the medical man). He leaves, surprisingly, the choice of the monumental inscription to his trustees, and leaves them £100 to maintain the grave, and that of his parents (at Charlton Park Cemetery). But ... 'if at any time my Trustees shall fail to apply the monies as hereinbefore provided', then the money was to go to Tonbridge School, to provide a bi-annual prize for an essay

> on the period from 750 AD to 1066 AD on any West Saxon King or on the period from 1066 AD to 1307 AD, the death of the greatest of the Plantagenets, Edward I, on any Norman and Angevin King 1066 to 1307.'

This emphasis will become significant.

The succeeding clauses deal with the various bequests. Clause V deals with his nephew, John Robin Owens, and section (b) directs

---

[4] Franklyn gave a talk ('illustrated by lantern slides') at the AGM of the Mid-Sussex and Eastbourne branch of the RSPCA in 1956, entitled *The Supreme Animal (felis catus)*. *Eastbourne Gazette*, 9 May, 1956. The *Sussex Agricultural Express* for 25 May 1956 notes that the talk had taken place, and that Franklyn was thanked by Lady Tollemache.

[5] It is not known if these requirements were ever followed, nor, if so, whether the grave is maintained – or where it is.

> that All my Academical Dress, gowns, robes, and caps, hanging
> in the left-hand side built-in cupboard in my bedroom, and
> Four silk or cloth hoods lying flat between tissue paper in
> the long drawer at the bottom of my gentleman's mahogany
> wardrobe in my bedroom, being MD, MA, and MB, BS, hoods
> expressing a wish that he should take care to preserve them
> free from moth, and that if some day his Son proceeds to a
> doctorate they may be treasured by him.

It would be interesting to learn what has become of them all. His Lausanne doctoral habit is in the Burgon Society archive, courtesy of Dr George Shaw, but the whereabouts of the rest is unknown. The four hoods were his London MB,BS, his Lausanne MD, his Malaya MA – and his Lincoln-Jefferson MA.[6] Thus 'MA' covers two degrees. They would, of course, be of use to his great-nephew only if he also proceeded to a doctorate in medicine at Lausanne, which he did not.

Clause VII deals with jewellery bequests. But it hides something more sinister. Section (a) details his bequests to his grand-niece Phillipa Anne Irene 'the blue-eyed fair-haired only daughter ...'. He goes on to 'express the devout hope that the man whom she marries eventually will have blue eyes so that she does not mix the races and that the next generation may be Saxons pure-blooded, blue-eyed, fair haired, as she is herself'.[7] In section (b), he expresses the 'same devout hope' for his grand-nephew, Nicholas Andrew: 'This point is of greater importance now to Nelson's country than ever before'. On the other hand, he also expresses a hope (not a 'devout' one, though) that he will never smoke, 'that being a foolish and unnecessary habit and lethal in effect if carried out over a long period of time'.[8]

Much of the rest of the Will is taken up with minute instructions about various heirlooms and how they are to descend within the family. There are copies of his various books – all 'rare', 'in much demand'. There are also two copies of *Family Récipés* [sic]: these go back to 1840, and Franklyn had them typed up and bound. They are 'of incalculable value'. A set of lantern slides – over one hundred – 'illustrating modern work in Heraldry and covering my work in this field 1922–1972': 'an unique collection' is to go to his nephew, or to the College of Arms if he does not want them.

The codicil, dated 23 May 1979, sets up two trust funds for his grand-niece. There was £5000 to be divided between them, the division to be at the trustees' discretion according to the needs of the first fund. The first was to enable her to obtain a royal licence 'authorising her to continue to bear

---

[6]This is known to have existed, as it is one of the hoods photographed by John Balsdon, and is shown in Figure 2 on page 32. It follows the Intercollegiate Code, with the university lining of purple with a wide white chevron, and has a binding of white velvet.

[7]See also page 20 above.

[8]This hope is occasioned by the bequest of a silver cigarette case given to CAHF by his parents, with the Franklin crest, and which he is bequeathing to his grand-nephew. In this case, we can agree with his judgment.

the Name and Arms of Owens and the Arms of Franklyn Quartered, united with the Arms to be granted or assigned or allowed to her Husband'. He then specifies that they shall be combined in quarters as follows:

> 1 and 4: Owens of Melksham and Cirencester.
> 2: Franklyn 'late of Jamaica and Antigua'.
> 3: her husband.

Furthermore, a pedigree was to be drawn up from the grandparents of her husband downwards, and 'proved and recorded' at the College of Arms. On top of this, the engagement is to be announced on the Court page of *The Times* and in the *Daily Telegraph*, and after the marriage has taken place, the trustees 'shall see that it is published also on the Court page of both papers and also in the Marriage columns (outside back page of *The Times*) and so on. And once the Royal Licence has appeared in the *London Gazette* two copies are to be obtained, she to keep one and the trustees the other.

> ... and in connection with the cost I request that her Husband should be invited to contribute towards the cost of granting Arms to his Family and the recording of his Pedigree as no doubt as a perfect gentleman he will naturally wish to do.[9]

All very fine and large, but if she does not apply for the royal licence, then she gets no money: £100 as a wedding present on the day, and the remainder of the capital of the fund. If she had not carried out the directions, then the money was to form part of his residuary estate. However, the second fund was to form an income for her for life, without condition. So again, there is a desire both to control things after his death, and the obsession with status and its trappings. One does wonder what would have happened had she married a non-armigerous man who refused to take out a grant of arms – indeed, that is something that is not known. The National Probate Calendar (Index of Wills and Administration) reveals that his estate was valued at £69 626.00.[10] This is worth in 2020 values about half a million pounds.

———

Obviously we cannot know what his legacy is within the family, or if indeed he is still remembered by them forty years later. But he has an important place in academic dress studies, if not always for the reasons he would wish.

---

[9]This is paralleled by a parenthesis in clause V.c of the main Will: he left his wine collection to his nephew John Robin Owens, '... so that he may at all times be able to serve a good vintage wine or champagne for a small lunch or dinner party. (This is one of the things that gentlemen should be able to do).'

[10]Volume for 1983, page 3407.

9 List of Publications

(This does not include his medical publications.)

Books

1. *The Bearing of Coat-Armour by Ladies*, John Murray, 1923
2. *University Hoods and Gowns*, a set of 25 large cards; WD & HO Wills, Bristol. 1926.
3. *A Short History of the Family of tiarks of Foxbury*, Adlard, London, 1929.
4. *The Genealogy of the Chavasse family*, 1929
5. *Short Genealogical & Heraldic History of the Families of Frankelyn of Kent and Franklyn of Antigua & Jamaica, B.W.I.*, London, E.O. Beck, 1933. (70 copies)
6. *A Genealogical History of the Families of Paulet (or Pawlett), Berewe (or Barrow), Lawrence, and Parker*, Foundry Press, Bedford, December 1963. (Printed privately, limited to 102 numbered and signed copies)
7. *A Genealogical History of the families of Montgomerie of Garboldisham, Hunter of Knap and Montgomerie of Fittleworth*, Ditchling Press, 1967.
8. Supplement to *A Genealogical History of the Families of Paulet (or Pawlett), Berewe (or Barrow), Lawrence, and Parker*, W. E. Baxter, Lewes, Sussex, December 1968. (Printed privately, limited to 150 numbered and signed copies)
9. *Academical Dress from the Middle Ages to the Present Day, including Lambeth Degrees*, W. E. Baxter, Lewes, 1970. (Printed privately, limited to 200 copies)
10. Frank W Haycraft, *The Degrees and Hoods of the World's Universities and Colleges*, 5th edition, revised and enlarged by Frederick R.S. Rogers, Charles A.H. Franklyn, George W. Shaw and Hugh Alexander Boyd, W.E. Baxter, Lewes, 1972. (Printed privately; 500 copies)
11. (with CEC Pontifex) *The family of Pontifex of West Wycombe, Co. Buckingham, 1500–1977*, Hassocks, 1977.
12. *The Genealogy of Anne the Quene (Anne Bullen) and Other English*

Families including Broughton of Impens, N. Petherton, Bridgwater, Co. Somerset, Pontifex of West Wycombe, Co. Buckingham, Wadding-ton of Mexborough, Co. York, Walwyn of Kilmersdon and Frome, Co. Somerset, and of Bognor Regis, Co. Sussex, together with a supple-ment to 'A Short Genealogical and Heraldic History of Four Families ...', 1977 (Printed privately, limited to 70 copies)

13. *The Ancient Family of Francklyn of Chart Sutton, Sutton Valence, Maidstone, Mereworth Castle, Kent Fotodirect*, 1977 (Printed pri-vately)

Articles

1. 'The armorial bearings of HRH the Duke of York, KG, and Lady Eliza-beth Bowes-Lyon', *The Illustrated London News*, 1923.
2. 'The new arms of the Duke and Duchess', Sphere, 1923.
3. Other articles in the *Pall Mall Gazette, Armorial Families*, and *Burke's Peerage and Landed Gentry*.
4. 'English and Scottish heraldry compared and contrasted', *Scots Maga-zine*, 1925.
5. 'The armorial bearings of HRH the Prince of Wales', *Graphic*, 1926.
6. 'Academic costume' in *The Oxford Magazine*, 6 and 13 February 1930: reprinted as a booklet.
7. 'The armorial bearings of HRH the Duke of Kent and HRH Princess Marina of Greece and Denmark', *The Illustrated London News*, 24 November 1934.
8. 'The Lambeth degrees', *British Medical Journal*, 12 October 1935.
9. 'Robes' in *Encyclopaedia Britannica*, 14th edition (1941 revision) and subsequent editions until 1970.
10. 'Academical dress: a brief sketch from the twelfth to the twentieth Century, with especial reference to doctors', *The Medical World*, 66, number 24 (31 July 1942) 465–68. Reprinted in *Oxford* 9:1 (Winter 1946/47) 78–85.
11. 'The chimere and convocation Habit', *Mid-Sussex Times*, 30 December 1942.
12. The coats-of-arms of the newly married couple' [sc: Princess Elizabeth and Philip Mountbatten], *The Sketch*, 26 November 1947.
13. With Rogers, FRS, 'Dress of the Clergy', a series of six short articles on aspects of clerical and academical dress, *Parson and Parish*, Nos 12–18 (October 1951–April 1953).

> I 'Introduction' (No. 12, pages 16–17);
> II 'Correct dress of bishops' (No. 13, pages 12–14);
> III 'Deans, archdeacons, canons, rural deans and priests' (No. 14, pages 27–28);
> IV 'Chimeres and habits' (No. 15, pages 27–30);

    V 'The hood and the almuce' (No. 16, pages 31–35);
    VI 'Processions' (No. 17, pages 29–30);

and in addition there are stinging replies by Franklyn and Rogers to two letters from correspondents who had the temerity to question points in earlier articles (No. 18, pages 20–21).

14. 'The arms of Princess Margaret and of her husband, Antony Charles Robert Armstrong-Jones, esquire', *The Illustrated London News*, 14 May 1960.

15. 'Academic dress, history of', in: *International Encyclopedia of Higher Education*, edited by Asa S Knowles, 10 vols (San Francisco: Jossey-Bass, 1978), volume I, 20–24.

Reviews

1. WN Hargreaves-Mawdsley, *A History of Academical Dress in Europe until the End of the Eighteenth Century*, Oxford 19:1 (December 1963) 102–04.

2. EW Scobie Stringer, *The Degrees and Hoods of the World's Universities and Colleges*, Theology 52 (1949) 232–33.

10 Timeline

1896	Born on 25 August at Brentwood.
1902	Family moves to Furze Hall, Horsell.
1904	Family living in Horsell (younger brother born).
1911	Family living in Hove.
1906	Goes to Edinburgh House Preparatory School.
1910	Goes to Tonbridge School.
1914	Goes to St Thomas' Hospital.
1915	January – Matriculates in the University of London.
	25 November – Starts military service in the Royal Garrison Artillery.
1919	9 February – Ceases military service; returns to St Thomas.
1921	Obtains BSc – Lincoln-Jefferson 'University'.
	Father dies.
1923	January – Admitted MRCS and LRCP; registered as a practitioner 23 January
	The Bearing of Coat-Armour by Ladies published; viciously reviewed.
1923–25	Locum GP.
1924	Graduates MB,BS(Lond).
	Obtains MA (Lincoln-Jefferson) (CF's first listing in *Medical Directory*).
1925	12 March – Graduates MD (Lausanne).
	Partner with CE Millington at Bickley until 1930.
1926	Writes text for Wills' cigarette cards of hoods.
1927	Living at Blackheath.
1929	Living in the Precincts of the Savoy.
	16 July – Marries Erica Bolton in the Savoy Chapel.
1930	6 and 13 February – *Academic Costume* published in *The Oxford Magazine*.
	Listed as partner in Boswell, Franklin, and Gilchrist in *Medical Directory*, 1930.
1931	Assists JGP Murray at Folkestone;
	living at 154 Sandgate Road.
1932	Changes spelling of name to Franklyn.

1933	March – Marriage annulled; address c/o Liskeard Gardens.
	March–December – MO on ship to Australia and back.
	Short Genealogical & Heraldic History of the Families of Frankelyn, etc published.
	December – Partner with DE Darbyshire at Lincoln.
	Living at The Corner House, 34 Queensway, Lincoln.
1934	Becomes also MO at Lincoln Prison.
	Has input into revision of Cambridge robes.
1937	January – Mother dies.
1938	Designs new scheme for 'Intercollegiate University'.
1939	MA *hon caus* 'Intercollegiate University'.
1940	October – Goes to Exeter College, Oxford.
1941	April – Leaves Oxford to return to medical practice.
	Buys Wickham Hill House.
	Takes on AD article in *Encyclopædia Britannica*.
1944 (?)	Designs robes for English Episcopal Church.
1945	Probably designs robes for 'Western Orthodox University'.
1946	9 December – Proposed second marriage announced.
1947	28 February – Second marriage called off.
1948	Has some input into Nottingham University robes.
	Designs robes for English Episcopal Church.
late 1940s	Advisor on AD to London College of Theology; designs hood.
1949	Designs Chichester Theological College hood.
	Designs University of Malaya robes.
1950	Probably designs Western Orthodox University robes.
1951	Designs Australian National University robes.
	Probably designs robes for 'Glastonbury degrees'.
	Awarded MA *hon caus* Malaya.
1952	Designs Southampton University robes.
	Probably designs Western International University robes.
1954	Designs Hull University robes.
1963	*A Genealogical History of the Families of Paulet* ... published.
	Attempts to get appointed to design Warwick University robes.
1964	Attempts to get appointed to design Essex University robes.
1968	Supplement to *A Genealogical History* ... published.
	Has input into New University of Ulster robes.
1969	11–22 August – Seriously ill in Westminster Hospital.
1970	*Academical Dress* published.
1972	*Degrees and Hoods*, 5th ed published – CAHF is one editor but effectively sole.
	Uses it to announce scheme for 'Independent University' – *sc* Buckingham.

	Hon DLitt first listed – on title page of *Degrees and Hoods*.
1977	*The Genealogy of Anne the Quene* published.
	The Ancient Family of Francklyn ... published.
1980	Moves to 44 Sackville Gardens, Hove.
198?	Moves to Old Fish Hall, Tonbridge.
1982	26 November – Dies. Buried at Putney.

.

11 Bibliography

Works by Franklyn are not listed, but are to be found in the list of his publications.

Primary Sources

- National Archives, Kew: Divorce Court File: 4553. Appellant: Charles Aubrey Hamilton Franklin. Respondent: Erica Milly Franklin otherwise Erica Milly Bolton. Type: Husband's petition for/of nullity.
- National Archives: Will of CAHF.
- University of Essex: correspondence in re academic dress.
- University of Hull: File of un-catalogued correspondence relating to the Academic Dress Committee (1953–55).
- University of London: digest of extracts of the Senate Minutes that deal with questions of academic dress from 1837 onwards.
- J Wippell & Co: file relating to the University of Hull (1953–55).

Secondary Sources

Periodicals

- *British Medical Journal*, passim.
- *London University Calendar*, passim.
- *Tonbridge School Register*, 1910.
- *The Medical Register*, passim.

Articles

- Richard Baker, 'The Academic Dress of the University of Hull from 1954 to the Present Day, Including the Hull–York Medical School from 2003', *Transactions of the Burgon Society* 11 (2011) 30–58.
- Arthur B Casey, 'Academic Dress: Personal Reminiscences', *Transactions of the Burgon Society* 8 (2008) 151–156.

- Nicholas Groves, 'Popularizing University Hoods and Gowns: Will's Cigarette Cards, 1926', *Transactions of the Burgon Society* 7 (2007) 48–74.
- Nicholas Jackson, 'The Development of Academic Dress in the University of Warwick', *Transactions of the Burgon Society* 8 (2008) 10–59.
- Alan J Ross, '*Togas gradui et facultati competentes*: The Creation of New Doctoral Robes at Oxford, 1895–1920', *Transactions of the Burgon Society* 10 (2010) 47–70.

Books

- Peter F Anson, *Bishops at Large*, Faber and Faber, London (1964).
- Charles Boutell, *English Heraldry*, Gibbings and Co., London (1899).
- Percy Dunsheath and Margaret Miller, *Convocation in the University of London, the First Hundred Years*, Athlone Press, London (1958).
- A C Fox-Davies, *Armorial Families: A Directory of Gentlemen of Coat-Armour*, seventh edition, vol. 2, Hurst & Blackett, London (1929).
- Nicholas Groves, ed., *Shaw's Academical Dress of Great Britain and Ireland*, vol. 1: *Degree-Awarding Bodies*, third edition, Burgon Society (2011).
- Nicholas Groves, ed., *Shaw's Academical Dress of Great Britain and Ireland*, vol. 2: *Non-Degree-Awarding Bodies*, third edition, Burgon Society (2014).
- William N Hargreaves-Mawdsley, *A History of Academical Dress in Europe Until the End of the Eighteenth Century*, Oxford University Press (1963).
- William N Hargreaves-Mawdsley, *A History of Legal Dress in Europe Until the End of the Eighteenth Century*, Oxford University Press (1963).
- Frank W Haycraft, *The Degrees and Hoods of the World's Universities & Colleges*, first edition, The Cheshunt Press, London and Cheshunt (1923).
- Frank W Haycraft, *The Degrees and Hoods of the World's Universities & Colleges*, second edition, The Cheshunt Press, London and Cheshunt (1924).
- Frank W Haycraft, *The Degrees and Hoods of the World's Universities & Colleges*, third edition, The Cheshunt Press, London and Cheshunt (1927).
- Frank W Haycraft, *The Degrees and Hoods of the World's Universities and Colleges*, ed. by E W Scobie-Stringer, fourth edition, The Cheshunt Press, London and Cheshunt (1937).
- Frank W Haycraft, *The Degrees and Hoods of the World's Universities and Colleges*, ed. by Frederick R S Rogers et al., fifth edition, W E Baxter Ltd, Lewes, Sussex (1972).

- George W Shaw, *Academical Dress of British Universities*, first edition, Heffer, Cambridge (1966).
- George W Shaw, *Academical Dress of British and Irish Universities*, second edition, Phillimore (1992).
- R Stevens, *Medical Practice in Modern England: The Impact of Specialization and State Medicine*, Yale University Press (2003).
- F M L Thompson, ed., *The University of London and the World of Learning 1836–1936*, Hambledon Press (1990).

The Burgon Society

The Burgon Society was founded in 2000 in response to a growing interest in the subject of academical dress. It is named after John Burgon (1813–1888), sometime Dean of Chichester Cathedral, Fellow of Oriel College, Oxford, and the only person to have a shape of academical hood named after him.

The aims of the society are:

- to coordinate the study of academical dress in all its aspects: design, history and practice;
- to preserve details of the past and present practices of institutions regarding academical dress;
- to act in an advisory capacity to film and television companies, and to those who wish to ensure correctness in the usage of academical dress.

Membership of the Society is open to anybody who is interested in academical dress. Fellowship of the Society is awarded to members on the successful submission of a suitable piece of original work.

The Society meets several times a year to receive newly submitted fellowship papers and to discuss other matters related to academical dress. It publishes a scholarly journal, *Transactions of the Burgon Society*, containing research papers submitted during the year; and organises exhibitions of academical dress and study visits. The Society also possesses a substantial collection of robes, and an archive of books and papers which are open, by prior arrangement with the Archivist, to anyone interested in undertaking research on academical dress.

If you would like to join the Burgon Society, please fill in the form at the Society's website www.burgon.org.uk. For further information, please email registrar@burgon.org.uk.

The Burgon Society is a registered charity in England and Wales (no. 1137522).